THE WAY OF LIGHT

The
Way of Light

THE PATH OF
NUR ALI ELAHI

Bahram Elahi

ELEMENT
Shaftesbury, Dorset ● Rockport, Massachusetts
Brisbane, Queensland

© Bahram Elahi 1993
Translation © J. W. Morris 1993

Published in Great Britain in 1993 by
Element Books Limited
Longmead, Shaftesbury, Dorset

Published in the USA in 1993 by
Element, Inc
42 Broadway, Rockport, MA 01966

Published in Australia in 1993 by
Element Books Limited for
Jacaranda Wiley Limited
33 Park Road, Milton, Brisbane 4064

Originally published as
Le Chemin de la Lumière
Albin Michel, Paris 1985

Cover photograph *Mountains* courtesy Pictor International
Cover design by Max Fairbrother
Designed by Roger Lightfoot
Typeset by Poole Typesetting (Wessex) Limited,
Bournemouth, Dorset.
Printed and bound in Great Britain by
Dotesios Ltd, Trowbridge, Wiltshire.

British Library Cataloguing in Publication
data available

Library of Congress Cataloging in Publication
data available

ISBN 1–85230–381–6

CONTENTS

Nothing of what is written in this book is mine. These are the teachings of my Master. All the discoveries are his, and I have only repeated what I heard and understood from him. May God forgive me if I have made any mistakes.

PREFACE

Nur Ali Elahi was born on 11 September 1895, in a village in Iranian Kurdistan. His father, Hajji Ni'matullah, was also a master of the spiritual path of the Ahl-i Haqq with a wide influence and following. In these favourable surroundings Nur Ali began to undergo the hardships of asceticism and spiritual discipline at the age of six, and his own spiritual rank qucikly became apparent. After the death of his father in 1921, Nur Ali left his spiritual retreat and moved to Tehran. Upon completing his studies he then worked as a judge in various cities in Iran. During that time very few people sought him out and benefited from his spiritual guidance. But gradually other seekers of the truth began to perceive the nature of his spiritual personality and faithfully followed his teachings. Since then his grace has touched a growing number of individuals from the most diverse backgrounds and origins. He wrote several books,[1] and his sayings were written down and published[2] by his son and disciple Bahram Elahi. His spiritual teaching has continued since his bodily departure from this world on 19 October 1974.

This book is a selection of lessons given orally by Bahram Elahi for small groups of French-speaking disciples in Iran and France between 1977 and 1986. It constitutes a deeper and more thorough treatment of some of the ideas outlined in his earlier book, *The Path of Perfection*,[3] inasmuch as the author's words here are intended for students of the path already seriously involved in spiritual practice. The question-and-answer format of the lessons has been preserved in order to reflect the spontaneity of the original discussions.

INTRODUCTION

Bahram Elahi, you were born in September 1931, and you grew up in Iran. Then you went to France for thirteen years to complete your medical studies and your specialization in surgery. And since 1964 you have again been living in Iran. What is your profession now?

I am currently a professor of pediatric surgery at the University of Tehran medical school. But with the help of God I find enough time to devote myself to spiritual matters. My love and respect for my profession have not made me forget that spirituality is absolutely fundamental in each person's life.

How did you become interested in spiritual matters?

When I was living in France I wasn't aware of spiritual matters in the way I am now. Of course I had faith in God; like everyone else around me I believed that He exists, but I didn't know why I believed that. Before that, when I was living in Iran, I performed my prayers and believed in God simply so that He would watch out for my personal interests; so I had a sort of materialistic relationship with God. That sort of belief was based on imitation and because I was afraid about my material interests: I thought that if I lost my faith I would lose everything else; it wasn't a spiritual matter. So when I went to France material life was so well taken care of from every point of view that I gradually lost that sort of faith. Since I didn't have any special material needs, I thought there was no longer any need for a Being to look after my material interests in life. I still had faith in God but I no longer felt any need for Him. I stopped performing my prayers and I simply had that faith, but nothing more.

But when I came back to Iran, in the Master's presence, I was inwardly transformed and I felt that I was no longer the same person as before. My life was illuminated by a different vision of religion and spirituality, an outlook I'd never had before. I loved God with an unshakeable faith that had awakened within me, a faith that was not motivated at all by any material interests. It was no longer a belief based on imitation, but a real faith grounded in immediate observation. I loved God because He deserved to be loved, because Love has been created for Him. I understood that the material world is impermanent and passing: whether you are a millionaire or poverty-stricken, in good health or bad – whatever state you're in, you realize that all this is only passing. Thanks to a light that entered my heart I felt and recognized that the spiritual worlds are infinite and everlasting. That's something you have to sense, to feel, like a light illuminating your heart; it can't be expressed in words. I saw that the spiritual world is eternal, while this material world is passing.

However, the material world still hadn't lost all its attraction for me, so I preferred to continue my material activities. But this luminous aspect of spirituality stayed with me and continued to attract me, and that spiritual attraction was so strong I felt forced to turn towards spiritual things and away from the material world without anyone else pushing me in that direction. Yet at the same time the material temptations and my carnal soul, my *nafs*, were still very strong . . . Ever since then I've been striving with all my energy to recognize the 'attractions' of the material world as they are in actual reality, not as we're taught to see and appreciate them. When you reach the point of seeing the material world as it really is, it truly has no attraction at all. Yet at the same time it's right just the way it is, and it's good that it's like that: without this material world no one would ever reach Perfection, no one would obtain the eternal divine grace.

Each person judges the world outside themselves according to their sensations and their own particular understanding. If you change inwardly, what is outside also changes for you. Everything you accomplish spiritually is done within yourself.

How is it possible for someone to change overnight the way you did, to suddenly move from a material to a spiritual vision of the world?
It was only later that I realized my angelic soul had changed as soon as I came back from France. If my inner outlook changed so totally, that was because I profited from the spiritual knowledge accompanying the new state of my soul. I understood what it meant to change one's spiritual soul: although I kept the same bodily habits as before, my perspectives and desires had changed; I had a different way of seeing things. Everything involving my body was the same, but everything involving my soul had changed.

How is that possible?
The changing of a soul isn't something common; it depends on the divine Will and Purpose.

Does it depend on the will of the individual concerned?
It depends on the divine Will. For example, there may be a particularly well-qualified body which is inhabited for a certain time by a soul that is not really worthy of that body, because of a particular accounting known only to God. Then when the right moment comes, God changes that soul.

Does one really have the impression of having completely changed?
You really do have the impression you've changed, that

you're no longer the same person. All my friends noticed that change. The next year, when I went back to France and saw my old friends, all of them told me I wasn't the same person as before. There wasn't one of them who didn't tell me that.

But did you yourself notice it right away?
I realized very quickly that my outlook and judgements had changed. For example, before then the other soul always wanted to get involved in material activities and loved money, success and ambition; the material world had an extraordinary attraction for that soul. Afterwards my body still felt that material attraction, but it was powerless in the face of what my soul desired. The light of that soul was stronger and dominated the wishes of my body, while the opposite had been true before, when my material desires had encompassed my spiritual ones.

Is there a relation between the fact that your soul was changed and the fact that you recognized your Master?
Yes, this transformation happened as soon as I saw my Master.

Was he the one who caused this change?
Certainly he intervened to help bring about this change. Authentic masters can do that . . . A perfect master is able to intervene and bring about this sort of change.

Didn't you already know your Master?
Yes, since he was my father.

Yet you never considered him to be your Master before this change in your soul?
His comportment was the same as it had always been, but I hadn't reached the stage where I could benefit from him . . . And I'm sure that would have been impossible, given the state my soul was in before that.

So you could say that it was through this change in your soul that you came to know your Master.

Yes . . . He was the same person, but I only gradually came to know and recognize his spiritual rank. It took me ten years to really come to know him. He did absolutely nothing that would make others suspect he was such an extraordinary being. Outwardly his behaviour was like that of an ordinary person. But once your inner perspective and outlook changed, the more you really came to know him, the more you saw that everything he did resembled a miracle.

Have you seen miracles?

Yes, very often. Once a person came to know him and no longer had any doubts about his spiritual rank and personality, then he would show himself; but otherwise he concealed them. He concealed those attributes from ordinary people, and he continued to do so until the end of his life. But for those who had faith in him he performed miracles according to the degree of their faith.

Yet I don't have the impression that the Master considered miracles and supernatural phenomena to be very important?

In principle the classical, spectacular miracles performed by the prophets, with God's permission, for the mass of common people were intended for unbelievers and those unacquainted with spirituality. Those individuals who have the divine light in their hearts have no need for miracles. As soon as they establish a relationship with their prophet or their saint – whether that be through seeing them personally or through reading and studying their works – they surrender themselves to the divine religion. Although they have no need for miracles their faith is strengthened by the miracles they witness. On the other hand those whose hearts have not been penetrated by the divine light – either because they are not yet prepared for that, or because their actions have deprived them of the capacity to receive that light –

remain untouched by miracles, indifferent to them, or even increase their hatred of God and His messengers.

But at a higher stage, for those who have completed the primary school of religion[1] and entered the path of perfection, miracles take a more subtle form. Those people see and sense in the person of their prophet, saint or authentic Master a continuous ongoing flow of miracles: a miracle, by definition, is something superhuman that the people of a given time are unable to accomplish by their own physical means.

Since these beings are linked to God or close to Him, miracles flow from them like water pouring forth from an inexhaustible fountain. This kind of miracle isn't intended for the masses; it is sensed, detected and understood by those who are spiritually awakened. It is like a great symphony: someone who knows and appreciates music understands what extraordinary things are accomplished in that work, while someone else may only hear the sounds without understanding, without grasping the miracle.

The people around Jesus didn't recognize that sort of miracle (except perhaps for his disciples); they only grasped the first, spectacular kind. The master also performed that sort of miracle.

What happened to the path after the Master's departure?
He maintains his contact with his spiritual school, through the intermediary of Hazrat-i Shaykh.[2]

Could you summarize in a few words the basic principles of the path of perfection?
1. Have faith in the One God.
2. Always be aware of God's presence with you, whatever your state and in everything you do.
3. Don't set yourself any particular spiritual goal, since the angelic soul's capacity for spiritual advancement is virtually unlimited. In other words carry out the divine commands as your duty, out of a sense of duty.
4. Seek only to please and satisfy God.

5. Combat the domineering self (the *nafs*) until your angelic soul controls it.

6. Whatever you think is good and wish to have for yourself, you should also wish for others; whatever you consider bad and reject for yourself, you should also reject for everyone else.

I am a student and a teacher at the same time. I have made an agreement to be a student of the Master, and he has entrusted me with the mission of teaching others in order to guide them. It is my duty to guide spiritually the person who comes seeking direction, to the extent of my knowledge and practical experience. Whether or not that person believes me depends entirely on the divine Will. If He wishes, that person will follow the path; but if He does not will it, you can try all the arts of rhetoric and persuasion and none of that will have any effect. It is not our duty to try to keep or to abandon any student: whether someone stays with the school or whether they leave depends entirely on Him.

I

BASIC PRINCIPLES

What is the basic work for a student in the school of spiritual perfection?

The fundamental task is to struggle against our domineering self (the *nafs*). Everything else has to do with the proper education of our way of thinking. Try to find the right training for your mind, because when we go to the other world we go there with our ideas, our way of thinking.

After death the soul has a course it must complete in order to advance toward its Beloved, Whom it is eager to rejoin. The soul's progress along this course gives it an ineffable feeling of ecstasy. The other world, the *barzakh*, is a world of tests and gradual advancement. While souls are going through those tests, which are like so many obstacles, the conditions and surroundings in which they are placed generally resemble those of life on earth. In principle, throughout the duration of the test the soul forgets that it is in the other world and feels as though it were back on earth. But as soon as the test is over, it again becomes conscious that it is in the state of an angelic soul in the other world. If it succeeds in passing the test, all the other souls congratulate it and it feels very happy. On the other hand, if it fails it senses their condescending looks and has a feeling of embarrassment and shame.

The person whose thoughts and ideas have been formed correctly passes these tests very easily and advances quite rapidly. But someone whose thoughts have been shaped by a bad or erroneous education – or even worse, who doesn't believe in God at all – gets nowhere and suffers as a result. These tests are for everyone, except for those who have reached Perfection or who have come to the end of their allotted period of fifty thousand years.

How should we go about doing this?
We have to educate and develop our thinking according to authentic spiritual teachings derived from a divine source, by means of our actions and our mental effort of auto-suggestion. But first of all we have to know the correct basic principles.

For example, if you learn a language from someone who pronounces it poorly, that bad influence will stay with you for the rest of your life. Or if you learn to play a musical instrument from someone who is unqualified, it will take a tremendous effort later to get rid of those bad habits.

In the case of spirituality as well, you have to have properly educated and developed ways of thinking, because a false idea can cause serious, sometimes irreparable, errors. For example, take the case of a person who arbitrarily decides that successive lives don't exist. Don't imagine that they will immediately discover their mistake as soon as they go to the other world. On the contrary, they won't understand at all. If their soul is good they'll be kept there and given certain lessons. So that soul will study those lessons and work for years in order to understand, and only at the price of enormous effort will they eventually come to understand each principle, such as the fact that successive lives do exist. Then they'll be brought back to this world once again. If they've learned their lessons well and passed the tests there, this idea will be engraved in their soul. So as soon as they hear about successive lives here they'll accept that notion without needing any further explanation. But otherwise someone will think such a thing is absolutely impossible, even if they hear about it for years on end. One has to suffer, go to a great deal of effort and overcome many obstacles in order to understand a single point.

The Master reported that Avicenna,[1] ever since his death, has been in the intermediate world (the *barzakh*) studying books in order to try to understand why the creatures are separated from God by different degrees of proximity or distance.

When a person goes to the other world, they see the realities corresponding to the education they gave their mind here. But if that person's thinking wasn't formed by a true and correct education they won't understand; they'll only feel the lack of that proper education. They'll notice with profound regret that others are farther ahead and are ascending much more quickly. They'll understand that they're ignorant and powerless, and they'll know that their salvation lies in true understanding.

We have to receive lessons, then learn and apply them. Everything depends on the proper education of our thinking. For example, this way of fighting the *nafs* and coming to control it is engraved in our mind; this is a case of 'educating your thinking'. In the other world, the soul awakens and becomes truly alive; but if you haven't worked spiritually here and if your ideas haven't been formed by a correct education, then you'll see everyone advancing while you remain stuck in the same place. It's like an athletics competition: you have to run, move ahead. Someone who hasn't done the right spiritual work is like a person who sees himself in a dream together with his friends and companions, who, having been liberated, are running up a hill to go back home. But that person himself, unable to advance, can only watch them move further and further ahead; despite desperate efforts, he's continually slipping behind and can't catch up with them.

Many people imagine that the other world is only an infinite space, that religion is just another philosophic question, and so on. But if they really knew that the other world is governed by precise and immutable rules and laws, that they will only receive there what they've come to deserve through their efforts in this world, then they would certainly work. For this earthly world is only a means for preparing our life in the other world.

How do you know that there is a life after death?
Man is a being with two dimensions. Our physical dimension has physical senses, and with those physical senses we are able to understand and grasp the physical world. But our metaphysical dimension, the angelic soul, also has its own particular senses, and those senses are intended for understanding and grasping the metaphysical world. So in order to establish a conscious relation between these two dimensions of our being, the self must first be purified and must therefore undergo a kind of 'spiritual purgatory'. In this respect people fall into three broad groups:

1. For those who have a conscious relation with their second, spiritual dimension, the existence of the other world is obvious and self-evident.
2. As for those who don't have any conscious awareness of their spiritual dimension, you can't make them accept the existence of something they don't even perceive. There's no point in trying to reason with them about this.
3. There are other people who do have a relation with their second dimension, but for whom that relation is vague and indistinct. You can reason with such individuals about spiritual things because there's something in them which confirms and agrees with that reasoning. And of course there are many intermediate degrees.

I know from experience that if you put the precepts of religion into practice and awaken your spiritual senses by struggles against the *nafs* (the domineering self), the things of the other world will be manifest and self-evident. (What is self-evident doesn't need to be shown by arguments; it needs the appropriate senses that are able to grasp it.) Then you will come to see and understand what I have understood, and if someone asks you the reason why, you'll answer: 'Go see for yourself . . .' For example, can you 'prove' that this lamp is turned on? That doesn't require a process of reasoning: you can see it yourself. But if I had no eyes and couldn't see, then you couldn't convince me that the light was turned on simply by reasoning and arguing about it. It's obvious, self-evident.

People ask me: 'What is the reason why you say the other world exists?' You can't answer such a question on that level. I respond: 'For the same reason you can see that there's light in this room.' These are obvious, self-evident things you can't arrive at by arguing: you feel them, perceive them, understand them with your spiritual senses. But if someone asks me: 'Since you've come to see these things, show me the way to follow so that *I* can reach that point too,' then in that case it is possible to show the way.

Don't pay any attention to people who say things like 'I have the truth and everybody else is wrong.' The truth is in each one of us, and God is everywhere. God will show the way to whoever relies wholeheartedly on Him and asks Him to show them the way. I don't believe in sects, or in anything else I can't see. I don't say it's false, nor do I say that it's true. I do say that God will take by the hand whoever wants God for His sake, and that He will lead that person where they need to go. But if someone wants God for the sake of something else, then they will have that other thing, but they won't have God. In other words, you have to become a sincere, genuine 'monotheist': to want God only for His sake, to see God everywhere, to think only of God, to see only God. It's not important whether you happen to be Protestant, Catholic, Muslim or Buddhist; what's important is that the original teachers of these religions were all prophets, all intermediaries sent to us by the One God.

Each human being is allowed to come back during a certain number of earthly lives in order to obtain the spiritual education that will allow them to reach perfection. The number of lives is limited. After a certain period of time they go to the other world and no longer have the right to come back to earth. They are judged there in the other world, and if they have earned nothing they will live on in a state of shame, remorse and regret. If they have obtained sufficient merit, for example by performing good deeds, then they gain a sort of spiritual 'capital' or reward. But if that person has properly educated their way of thinking, they will be able to reach perfection. So if they have some spiritual 'capital', like those Christians or Muslims who perform good actions in order to obtain paradise, then they will go to paradise.

But all of that is still below perfection. Perfection is something else: it requires spiritual study, having the proper education of your mind and way of thinking. Those are the people who reach perfection. If you don't work spiritually in this life you'll have to work at it in another lifetime, and so on throughout the number of lives that are available to you. And when they're over you will go to the other world permanently, without coming back.

(If someone tells me that they don't believe what I'm saying, that doesn't matter. Each person acts to save their own soul, but it is our duty to respond when someone asks us questions . . .)

Of course the soul doesn't necessarily have to spend the full fifty thousand years on earth: the person who attains perfection, or even someone whose thinking has reached a certain degree through education, no longer has to come back to earth; they continue their path in the other world. Fifty thousand years is the maximum allowable period, but of course it can be reduced for certain individuals who have made a special effort.

Some people say: 'But it's very good to come back to earth, why not come back to this world?' The Master said: 'Once you've been in the state of 'soul', you won't say that any more. Even those who are in hell have no desire to come back to earth.'

If a person doesn't manage to reach their assigned goal during the period of fifty thousand years, then it is finished until the resurrection and the day of the final judgement. After that it will all be over. This is why I always advise my friends not to fall back, not to stop or go astray, not to do any negative things. And as for myself, I would prefer to be an atheist rather than follow a false master or a false religion. Because when you're an atheist, at least you are at point zero; but if you follow a false master or a false religion you fall into the negative zone.

Those who follow a false master or false religion do not seek God for God's sake. Instead they want God for the sake of a certain personal interest, pleasure, enjoyment or power. There is none of that at all in the authentic religions. What did Jesus offer humankind? Neither spiritual amusements nor material advantages. Likewise with Muhammad, and with Moses too, although he did proclaim the 'promised land'. But Jesus didn't do that. For a Christian, the best example of charity and surrender to God is the life of Jesus – although there are some things in it that shouldn't be taken literally. For example, if Jesus didn't get married that was because he had no inclination to do so; he didn't have sexual desires.

What are the logical reasons why we have fifty thousand years in order to reach perfection?
The number isn't important. What is important is that the limit is the same for each person, and that everyone has the same period of time available. Otherwise, how could there be any divine justice?

What happens to the soul between the time it leaves the body and the time it comes back to inhabit a new earthly body?
Except for certain special cases, it necessarily goes to the intermediate world (the *barzakh*). If the soul has had faith in God or if it has lived according to its conscience, it has a feeling of great relief at having left the body. In fact everyone, even a terrible sinner, feels a sense of relief at leaving earthly life. It's as though they were suddenly released from

a heavy burden they'd been carrying throughout a long journey. Thus for those who have faith and who've led an upright life, death is a deliverance: the farther the soul has advanced and ascended and the more it is fully conscious and filled with faith, the more its experience of death is pleasant and the more deeply it feels that liberation and that exalted sense of well-being. And if the soul has reached the end of its process of perfection it experiences a feeling of ineffable ecstasy at the moment of death.

When a person dies, ordinarily the soul spends a certain time in the places where that person lived, and it may even attend the funeral ceremonies. After that it meets the souls of those it has loved during its previous earthly lives. Others may encounter saints, prophets or other luminous beings who take them and lead them to the intermediate world – and there the soul, whatever its rank and degree of understanding, experiences an extraordinary sensation of awakening. The first thing that is examined after the soul's arrival in the intermediate world is its degree of true faith. The soul may stay in that intermediate world (*barzakh*) only a second, or it may remain there for many years. It may even be able to stay there and continue its process of perfection without having to return to earth: in the *barzakh* it works in joy, without pain; since it is freed from the weight of the earthly body and its needs, it feels nearer to God's presence.

Everything you can think of exists in that world, and everything you can't imagine exists there too. During a certain time the soul maintains its ties with its earthly acquaintances. In general, the period of each person's stay in the intermediate world is related to the consequences of their earthly actions and to the level of spiritual education of their way of thinking.

Can a soul that has reached perfection ask to come back to earth or be sent there again in order to increase its degree of perfection?
The earth is an extremely low place for the soul, and often even ordinary souls do not want to go back there. So you

can easily understand why a soul that has reached perfection would not want to return to earth, except for certain souls of a very high level which have the same rank as the archangels or even higher. Such special souls do come down to the earth for certain missions and then return where they came from once their mission is completed. This particular movement or coming-and-going of these special souls of extremely high rank is called a 'circular' motion.[2] Which is to say that they don't actually advance from one degree to the next, since they have already reached their highest possible rank, but they do win a special honour or merit. But as for us ordinary souls, we are moved in both ways, by 'circular' and 'linear' advancing motions.

Can a soul go to other planets?

A soul destined for a given planet can't go to other planets (except for certain special cases) as long as it hasn't completed the specific time-period that has been prescribed for the souls of its own planet. For example, that period is fifty thousand years for the earth; so an earthly soul cannot go to other planets until that fifty thousand years is up. Of course there are many other inhabited planets besides our earth.

Are all souls equal?

They differ according to their capacity, their type, etc . . . You may understand better if we compare the essence of each soul to a weight: one soul, for example, might weigh a hundred grams, while another weighs only a gram, but both souls have the same characteristics, both of them can reach their perfection and both can rejoin God.

You mean they differ according to their capacity?

That term isn't really adequate; a great number of different factors taken together all affect this 'capacity'. These capacities can't be defined in rigid, textbook fashion. Let's simply say that the soul of Jesus, for example, is different from the human soul of an ordinary person. But that ordinary person can still advance and reach a high rank.

One has the impression you consider some beings to be 'inferior' and others to be 'superior' . . .

The differences I'm talking about are not the kind of differences you're thinking of: they have to do with degrees of proximity and distance from God. Each soul's relative closeness or distance from God depends on a great many factors. One of these is that soul's actions, but of course there are other factors as well. For example there may be certain people who don't really know themselves yet – that is, who are not fully aware of their true spiritual situation and who have fallen into an unfavourable *milieu* as a result of specific spiritual accounts, or because of their past record. Therefore we can't rely on criteria like outward behaviour, surroundings and social position by themselves in order to gauge a person's spiritual worth: you have to know and truly understand the inner being, the soul of each person in order really to know who they are and what is their spiritual rank. Needless to say, those who are near to God, even if they don't yet fully know themselves, still have no desire to do bad things, to commit major sins and the like. For example, they are unable to commit a crime; they obey the voice of their conscience, even without knowing why.

What is the difference between the human soul and the divine Essence?

The divine Essence is what is absolutely immaterial. Every angelic soul has a particle of it, since otherwise it would die. It is a particle of God, and it is immortal. We have to distinguish between what is relatively immaterial and what is absolutely immaterial: the human soul, the *jinn*, the angels are relatively immaterial. Only God is absolutely immaterial.

Therefore everything besides God is material?

We don't really have words capable of clearly expressing what I just mentioned, because the words we use can't convey these realities very precisely. If we take as our starting point the fact that God is absolute Purity, then every creature in creation must have a certain 'impurity'. Since we don't have a better term, I've used the word 'material'.

If everything material must eventually disappear, what does that mean for the promises of eternity, of an eternal life in hell and paradise?
Truly eternal life is for those who have reached perfection.

Do you mean there is a 'relatively' eternal life?
Eternal . . . You could say it is relative, except for God and those who have joined Him.

People say that things 'die'. But in reality nothing disappears: all the elements decompose and are transformed, but they don't totally disappear.
That depends on whether God wants what He created not to disappear. In principle, He doesn't return it to nothingness.

Otherwise it would be absurd!
God, by definition, does not do anything absurd . . .

There are some readers of The Path of Perfection[3] *who don't understand it, while others find the book extremely clear and are guided by it.*
It isn't a book that will be accepted by everyone: it will please some people and leave others indifferent. It is a book of pure spirituality and a guide for those individuals who are concerned about their destiny in the other world – above all for those who have already covered a certain distance on the spiritual path and who are still seeking the answers to a wide variety of problems. If they read it perhaps they will find

their answers. But other people who aren't yet concerned about their destiny in the other world, or who have had few or no spiritual experiences, will remain uninterested.

In addition we mustn't forget the factor of the spiritual atmosphere today. Unfortunately our age is dominated by a negative spiritual atmosphere. We must hope that God will change that atmosphere in the direction of greater light as soon as possible. For there are certain people who understand the book, and others who are like sheep, who are just followers. Do you see what I mean? If this age weren't dominated by the negative forces, a large enough number of people would understand, and then the others would follow.

What about those who are seeking the truth, but who don't believe in God: are they still guided by their angelic soul anyway?

You could say that they aren't, since if the influence of their angelic soul were really dominant it would have led them above all to believe in God. Such people do manage to realize a great many truths, but there are always certain things they won't understand because they've neglected the most essential foundation. They want to act according to their conscience, but what is the origin of the laws and precepts of their conscience? Our conscience is a foundation, something we've been entrusted with so that it can be educated. That is why God's messengers were sent to educate people's consciences in the right direction, the direction for which the conscience was originally created.

Those who are unacquainted with spirituality think that it's nothing but a matter of social convention.

It may also have a conventional value – but here we are involved with religious convention.

But aren't there any eternal truths?

There are eternal truths, but most people aren't able to grasp them. If these things seem conventional to certain people, that's all right with us: they think we're 'conventional', and we are on God's side; they have their own outlook, and later we shall see who was right. In reality it's God who tells us that lying is bad, and therefore we don't lie. Yet certain groups think lying doesn't matter, as long as their desires are satisfied. But in reality the divine precepts are not conventional; they are divine commands and true realities.

Isn't the truth relative, even for perfect souls?

The perfect soul sees the pure Truth, the absolute Truth, but according to the limits of its capacity. Of course other truths also exist which surpass the limits of that soul's vision. Its vision is limited because God alone is the absolute Truth. The power and the knowledge of every other creature, even of the archangels, is limited and relative; there are things that even the archangels don't know. But someone who is perfect no longer feels any need: their cup has become full, and they have no wish to change places with anyone. The other world is a distinctive sensation or awareness (a *kay-fiyat*):[4] you have to go there in order to understand it, and you have to reach perfection in order to understand perfection.

You speak of perfection in terms of knowledge and understanding, not in terms of happiness.

Happiness is one aspect of knowledge and understanding; when you have absolute knowledge and understanding you have everything. But you can have happiness without understanding . . . Of course I'm speaking about spiritual understanding, and not formal knowledge.

What distinction are you drawing between formal knowledge (savoir) and true understanding (connaître)?

With respect to spiritual matters, everyone knows, but almost no one really understands, because true understanding is formal knowledge put into practice, tested and exper-

ienced by the individual himself. It is this personal experience that awakens the soul. The *sophia* of the Greeks, the
nirvana of the Buddhists, and *ishrâq* (illumination, enlighten-
ment) in Islam all correspond to this awakening. You can
learn all sorts of things, but you only really understand
when, through putting them into practice, you actually
come to grasp the true reality of a thing (if it has such a
reality). For example, I may 'know' the definition of sugar;
but as long as I haven't tasted it myself I don't truly know its
taste. There are authentic, true spiritual writings and false
ones, and it's only through personal experience that you can
distinguish between them, just as you would distinguish
between true and false sugar by tasting them. Or take
another example: I 'know' what America is, but I don't
really know it from experience. In order to really know and
understand it you have to go and live there.

*You've written that: 'If someone possesses full spiritual know-
ledge, then that person implicitly knows all the material sciences as
well.'[5]*

Of course. A perfect human being, according to the
definition we've given, must know everything, to the
extent of their perfection. When I say 'everything', that of
course includes the spiritual plane as well as the material
plane, since the material sciences are also derived from spiritual knowledge. But people rarely think of that aspect of the
problem: an inventor usually thinks that he is the one who
has made a discovery, whereas in reality his formula has
already been, as it were, written down or created in the
spiritual world; only after that does he come to discover it
here. The Master once said that the formula enabling people
to remain youthful had been written down ten years earlier,
and that someone would perhaps discover it in thirty or
forty years. The person who discovers that formula will
believe that he's the one who invented it, although it has
already been known for fifty years in the spiritual world. In

reality that scientist will only have grasped an idea which was already widespread in the atmosphere.

You say that all the forces of creation are within the human being, but I don't have the impression that the students of the path of perfection are seeking to discover them.

What do you mean, they aren't seeking? As soon as they begin to advance along the path of perfection those things automatically become clearer to them. They don't need to look for them, because they will see. The higher they climb, the further they will be able to see. Do you understand? They don't need to look for them outside themselves, because everything is within each of us.

You write that a person only becomes perfect when they have passed through and understood everything that exists in creation. Does understanding here imply personally experiencing everything?

Yes, but there are two ways to understand or experience things. You can experience something step by step, as it were, like an ant who walks along and sees each thing point by point. Or else you can make a sudden spiritual 'leap' up high and see things with a higher, comprehensive spiritual vision, without having to experience every detail. This doesn't mean that such people don't have any experience, but rather that they don't have to experience everything individually. There is a horizontal, level way to go, and there is a 'vertical' way. If you want to really know a territory there are two ways of viewing it: you can examine it 'horizontally', which takes a great deal of time and doesn't give you a comprehensive outlook; or you can approach it 'vertically', meaning that the higher you climb, the clearer, more precise and more comprehensive your vision becomes. That's why people speak of the movement of spiritual perfection in terms of 'ascension' and progression.

What do you mean by 'earthly experiences'?

'Earthly experiences' means, for example, that it's necessary for us to know directly all the animal attributes existing in our self, and that we have to have them in our self. In other words, we have to know lust, lying, theft, hatred, malice, anger . . . to know what they are. When I speak of earthly life I'm referring to all the *basharic*[6] qualities that are within us, because the *bashar* is a complete animal, a 'perfect animal', if you will.

Now there are two kinds of trials or experiences:

1. There are those the *sâlik*[7] voluntarily establishes for himself, such as performing a fast or helping the poor. This is easy to do.
2. There are those God imposes on each person. These trials are very difficult, and they're extremely displeasing to the carnal soul (the *nafs*). But if someone passes this kind of test that is excellent, and that person gains God's satisfaction.

In principle, each time the *sâlik* sets up a trial for himself in addition to his usual duties, that brings on a similar trial sent by God, as a result of the process of 'action-and-reaction'. You have to expect such a trial: every time you wish to go beyond your duties and do too much, a trial of this sort comes from God. Most often the uninformed disciple fails this second sort of test. For in principle, if such a voluntary test is motivated by ostentatious pride and pretentiousness and not by the desire to come closer to God, the divine trial sent as its consequence will cause the person to fail in their path. An authentic Master can neutralize the negative effect of the failures following from such trials, because the divine Grace intervenes through the Master's intercession. But if you have no Master this sort of trial will cause you to fall . . .

One has the impression, in reading sacred writings, that the saints put more stress on our duty to serve God, rather than on the duty of seeking to know Him. But you seem to say the opposite.

There is no difference between the two: how could you

pretend to come to know God without serving Him? There are many popular stories about the saints, but people don't really know the saints: what you have seen is their outward aspect. The saints only revealed a small portion of the truth, under the penalty of . . . But read the biographies of the saints and you'll understand what I mean! No one has the right to reveal divine secrets without God's permission. If He had so desired there wouldn't be this separation between the metaphysical self and the physical ego, there wouldn't have been this forgetfulness of our previous lives. That is why the saints and divine messengers most often speak in a symbolic manner, in the form of parables.

The Master says that the highest form of devotion is to serve others, not to acquire knowledge.

Yes, and Jesus Christ says the same thing. When you reach true inner knowledge, then you will also understand what you ought to do, what is really best. You say that the best thing is to serve others, but *how* should we serve them? Tell me that. First you have to *know* how to serve. Serving others is one of the actions that allows you to gain true knowledge. So knowledge and understanding determine everything; everything flows from that. If you don't really know, how can you pretend to act properly? In order to understand, you have to know yourself; and if you don't know yourself, how can you serve others in the way God wants you to?

Where does evil come from?

Nothing that comes from God is bad. Evil is a complication resulting from our misguided actions.

Does a force of repulsion exist?

Each created being has an inner property of returning toward its Creator. The force of repulsion only exists where there is a certain free will and choice, as in the case of the human being. A force of repulsion against evil exists in each of us: we must educate it and combat the evil in ourselves and for others.

What do you mean by 'negative forces'?

When you feel an attraction towards God, for example, that is a positive force. But conversely, there are also negative forces. It doesn't really matter where they come from. They attack the person whose faith is feeble, just as germs attack the person whose body has been weakened. People are susceptible to those forces, although they don't realize it. The domineering self (*nafs*) feeds on those negative forces, and we ourselves may be affected by them. Otherwise it would be easy to combat the *nafs*, if it were all alone . . . If the *nafs* is not reinforced by these external forces it is easier to fight against it.

There are two kinds of negative forces: one of them, the domineering self or *nafs* (with its characteristics of vicious animals), is within us; the other kind, which is outside us, is the group of spirits whose mission is to turn us away from the right path by acting in conjunction with our *nafs*. Nor should we forget the influence of negative human beings.

What do you mean by spiritually 'negative' people?

Those are people who are controlled and dominated by negative spirits, and who attack and criticize authentic spirituality. They can be either aware or unaware of their condition, and they belong to several different categories. The most dangerous of these negative human beings are those who take on an outwardly spiritual colouring and remain unaware of their condition.

We must distinguish between two sorts of attacks on religion. There are attacks regarding certain points that are not authentic, but which only concern the 'religions of men'. That sort of attack is justified and is not a bad thing. On the other hand, attacks directed against the authentic aspects of religion and against spiritual truths are unforgivable.

The seriousness of this sort of spiritual negativity depends on several factors. First, with regard to the person who actually carries out these attacks, there is (a) the spiritual 'account' they've accumulated during their preceding lives; and (b) the spiritual knowledge and understanding they've gained during this life. For example some people attack religion because they were born into a social *milieu* hostile to spirituality; that is one of the consequences of acts they committed in preceding lives. Others who attacked religion during an earlier life become the followers of false religions. Secondly, there are factors involving the spiritual level and particular religious personalities someone criticizes. For example, to attack the level of exotericism – as with atheists and materialists who deny God and religion in general – is less serious than to criticize the esoteric dimension of religion. To attack an authentic spiritual school is even more serious, and the gravest fault of all is to attack those who have been specially sent or designated by God.

There have been a great many traitors in history, but Judas' betrayal of Jesus remains the classic example. The case of Yazîd[8] was different because he wasn't aware of Husayn's spiritual personality; his misdeed was the outcome of other acts committed during his previous lives. But Judas had recognized the reality of Christ, since he later repented. And yet all he did was to sell Jesus by pointing him out to his enemies. But there are even worse cases, as when a disciple directly and personally attacks and abuses someone close to God . . .

How is it possible for the disciple of an authentic Master to become transformed into a spiritually negative person?

The divine law demands that contrary qualities always be in contact with each other. Disciples who set out on the spiritual path should know that innumerable dangers, both visible and invisible, are awaiting them. Their only chance of safely reaching their goal lies in taking the hand of a true, experienced spiritual Master and then in following that Master with steadfast determination, without letting themselves be distracted and without paying attention to anything but their Master's guidance.

As long as the disciples vigilantly maintain the connection with their Master they will remain out of danger.

What are the typical characteristics of spiritually negative persons?

Spiritually negative individuals can be recognized by several traits:

1. Like chameleons, they outwardly take on the spiritual colouring that is present in the *milieu* they are attacking.
2. They use every means at their disposal to make themselves likeable and agreeable in terms of the corresponding weak spots of those they wish to contaminate. But their actions don't live up to their words.
3. They always defend a dead person, never someone who is living. (Or if they favour a living person, it's a 'master' who's actually their puppet.) When they are preaching for themselves, they superficially copy the outward aspect of the spiritual figure they claim to follow. They are unaware that each true Master has his own particular spiritual personality, corresponding to the development of his particular time and social environment. Hence they don't succeed in imitating their model on both the material and spiritual planes. For example, someone may claim to be like Christ, but that person won't manage to have at the same time Jesus' chastity, poverty and ability to perform miracles.
4. They have no fear of God. The first step for a spiritually negative person is that they lose their faith and their fear of God. Someone who fears God, even if they don't follow a spiritual path, will never attack religion. The person who fears God is in dread of the final judgement. Because they are concerned about their spiritual destiny

they're afraid to do anything that could harm their life in the other world, and so they listen to the voice of their conscience. Whenever they're tempted they take the necessary precautions in order not to commit an irreparable sin; so even if such a person is tempted to attack spirituality they'll say to themselves: 'But what if that turned out to be true?'

5. They are full of pride; pride keeps them from submitting to God. They also have an uncontrollable weakness for certain earthly attractions. Both of these traits predispose certain disciples to fall into the traps of false masters or else to break off their spiritual connection if they're already following the path of a true Master.

What is the process that eventually leads a disciple to break his or her spiritual connection?

At first the disciple only participates passively, by lending an ear to negative and hostile remarks. That helps make the soul inactive and weakens the spiritual defences. The negative force is like a colourless, odourless gas that can drug a person without their ever being aware of the fact.

This sort of criticism begins by attacking the people around a Master and gradually approaches him more directly. Then the *nafs* becomes more active and starts to criticize everything; it even goes so far as to criticize God. It eats away at the person's spiritual connection like a mouse gnawing on a rope. Or certain individuals may cut their connection with a single blow.

How can we protect ourselves against that?

Fanaticism is a bad thing, and we disapprove of it; but in this particular case we must rely on a very special form of zealousness directed against our own domineering self (*nafs*). This is not the ordinary sort of blind, outward fanaticism directed against others, but a peculiar form of intentional, purely internal zealousness which we ourselves must direct against our domineering self. This inner attitude helps create a protection against the penetration of negative forces, and at the same time it also constitutes an excellent starting point for nurturing the pure Love of God.

The religions say that 'the devil' exists . . .

Devils (in the plural) do exist. In addition to the domineering self, there are also devils. First of all there is the diabolical force, but there are also diabolical individuals. The diabolical force can flow from either the domineering self (the *nafs*) or from diabolical individuals who may be either visible or invisible: the invisible ones are the *jinn*, while the visible ones are human beings who have transformed themselves or changed themselves into devils.

Without the domineering self to receive these influences, the devil would not be able to have any effect on us. In the Qur'an (15:42) God says to Satan: 'You will never have any power over the hearts of My true servants.' The external devil is an active force, but if there is nothing in us to receive that force the devil can't affect us. In the story of Job, where it is said that the devil in person intervened, with God's permission, that is only to help us understand the role played by the domineering self . . .

Let's suppose that an external devil does exist: if you don't have the domineering self to receive those forces, it's as though he didn't exist. If someone lacks the sense of taste, then for that person tastes simply don't exist. For someone without hearing, sounds don't exist. If the domineering self doesn't run us, if *we* control *it*, then the devil doesn't exist – or rather, although he does exist, he can't influence us. So we are able to jump ahead to another stage. Needless to say, the external devil *does* exist, but he can only act through the intermediary of our domineering self.

Therefore it is our responsibility to gain control of our 'receiver' (the *nafs*) so that we can neutralize the harmful effects of those negative forces.

Can we know who those diabolical souls are?

Souls are not diabolical in themselves: they can have a particular mission to bring about plagues and calamities, accidents and other distressing and disastrous events. There is also a certain group of pure and very exalted souls, like the angel of death, who have the divine mission of bringing down catastrophes for humankind. When those catastrophes are sent by God they are controlled by certain lofty souls in the other world. For example, it is said that when God wanted to wipe out the *jinn* He sent an army of angels, or in the story of Lot, where it is angels of light who send down the earthquakes and fire from heaven.

Diabolical souls influence us through our domineering self, our *nafs*. Those human souls who have a particular maleficent divine mission are very advanced souls. On the other hand, the souls of people who've transformed themselves into devils are not free to harm others; they have no power, because the power of an angelic soul is directly proportional to its degree of purity and perfection. Those who've become devils are wretched souls burning with the unhappiness and misery of regret for occasions they let slip by, or suffering from other punishments. There are also special instances where the souls of evil people, under certain conditions, are allowed to demonstrate their evil character to the living; but that is not the general rule.

Are there diabolical souls in places devoted to dissolute, immoral activities and the like?

Yes, because places where the spiritual atmosphere has been polluted by lust, crimes, forbidden activities and things like that attract those ill-intentioned, diabolical spirits.

So does this mean that people aren't responsible for their actions, that the devils are in control?

No, people are responsible. Why should they fall under the influence of their surroundings? They have done certain things in the past, and so they have to fall under that influence. But why are you yourselves not controlled by that influence? The negative force is so overwhelming that many people can't resist it. However, I do know that if only they would cry out to God, He would hear them and save them. But they don't have any desire to cry out; that doesn't interest them and they scoff at it. The devils are controlling such people, but it is the divine, positive forces who allow them to have that influence; it is necessary for them to be in control for a certain period. If the positive Force made a single gesture they would be wiped out, so it is only with Its permission that they're in control. It is a trial, it is more than a simple misfortune; it is a spiritual calamity for the people of our time. And it is a terrible misfortune because they've lost their faith, because they don't have faith. They have technology, material goods and pleasures, and all the rest. But they don't have faith.

Everything here comes from Above. So right now, if you notice that they've let the devils loose, that is because they were released up There. It is our misguided and evil actions that have created this favourable occasion for them, that have made this their age. So they've won the right to rule our spiritual atmosphere for a certain time.

Is this the normal path that human beings have to follow?

People haven't wanted the prophets and saints. Most of them have been martyred and persecuted, and their words have been lost or corrupted. So people came to deserve God's establishing the rule of devils. Now it is time for them to cry out with all their hearts for the prophets and saints to intervene. There are people who have truly started to cry out. And there are a lot of them. Everywhere in the world there are individuals who have awakened, who are fed up with this spiritual atmosphere and this way of living. Their hearts are crying out, and when the number of those cries reaches a certain threshold, that is the moment when the positive forces will reappear and reverse the current spititual atmosphere.

But what if they don't cry out for God?

But they're already crying out; the heart can only cry out to God. It's sufficient if a society comes to be fed up with something. When a person is fed up with a particular situation their heart transmits something.

Does this mean that people in the past were more advanced?

Let's assume that by 'in the past' you mean the cycle of civilization of the most recent Adam, because according to the Imam Ali there have been an astronomical number of successive 'Adams' since the creation of the first Adam. In the past people were simpler, but the spiritual atmosphere was more conducive to faith. In our own time people's way of thinking is more highly developed, but the spiritual atmosphere has become very detrimental to faith. The person who can still practise true religious belief today gains an extraordinary honour and will be singled out among the other souls in the spiritual world. The Master said: 'Those who succeed in keeping their faith during this era will earn a special distinction among the souls.'

What sort of people will not have any intercessor with God?

Those who commit deadly sins without being forced to do so, who act without remorse and while knowing that they are committing a deadly sin.

What is the 'divine Regard'?

There is a spiritual law that has been called the 'divine Regard'. The divine Regard is a special manifestation of God's Grace, Compassion and Kindness. At every instant it watches over the person who is the object of this privilege and protects them against every sort of danger. It warns that person about their mistakes in order to keep them from straying from the right path, and it helps them to see their good actions in order to encourage them. That person feels the presence of an omniscient Guide who watches over them and directs them with loving kindness, compassion and deep affection. The divine Regard allows that person to grow spiritually: like a rose, they open up and blossom in the radiance of the divine sun.

When someone denies God and spirituality, God removes that person from His Regard. He no longer looks out for them, and He abandons them to their own devices so that they receive no spiritual warnings. As a result that person wanders aimlessly, intoxicated with their material success, drowning deeper and deeper in sin and denying God, spirituality, the metaphysical world, the final judgement, and all the rest. They have no fear of God.

Such individuals, blinded by their pride, say: 'Who has seen the other world? Everything is just fine right here, and we ought to indulge our pleasures to the greatest possible extent . . .' So God turns His Regard away from them and lets them pile up the heavy burden of their sins to the point where they can no longer be saved, because on the day of judgement no saint or redeeming prophet will defend them or want to take care of them. But without an intercessor, who will help them answer for their deeds if no one is willing to help them? It will be too late, and they will have to suffer all the consequences of their actions, because then they are subject to the divine Justice. When I think of the vast number of errors and sins that even a pious individual unconsciously commits every day, I shudder at the fate of people like that. The prophets and saints asked God in their prayers to save them from His Justice on the day of judgement – since even they feared having to answer before it – and instead asked Him to look upon them with His Regard of Grace and Compassion. So given that, you can understand what those beings who are subject to the divine Justice must have to suffer!

Most people are unaware of the deeper meaning of religious words and precepts, and don't realize that religion can only be actualized through personal experience. Thus when someone speaks about the divine Wrath and Justice, those who have had a direct personal experience of religion and whose spiritual senses have been awakened shudder at the very words, while other people simply hear them without grasping the meaning they conceal. For example, those who have lived through war and its horrible sufferings shudder whenever they hear someone talk about a new war. But for other people war has a purely verbal meaning that only penetrates the most superficial layer of their consciousness.

False masters who deceive people – and all those who in any way deal with religion and use it for a purpose that is not divine, whether to gain a reputation, to acquire a certain social position, to become wealthy, etc – all such persons ought to realize that the divine Justice really is awaiting them. When they appear before the divine court, they will have to answer first of all to God for having falsified His commandments, for having invented precepts they attributed to Him, or for having hidden certain truths in order to protect their personal interests. Then they have to answer before the prophets, saints and true spiritual Masters for having falsified their path. And finally, they will have to respond to the accusations of all the people they have deceived and have led down false paths. In addition, the false masters and false guides will have to answer for having guided people without any divine authorization or mission.

To play with religion and spirituality is the single most dangerous thing a person can do, since it can eventually have disastrous, sometimes irreparable and even eternal consequences. When someone commits a misdeed they're only held accountable for that particular action, and that person is only responsible for himself. But when an individual takes on a responsibility for other people, whether spiritually or materially, then that person is held accountable for all of them and for all the errors and misdeeds they commit under his influence. The same law also applies in the positive direction: those who encourage people toward a spiritual or material good will be rewarded for the good things which others accomplish as a result of their encouragement and direction. The path of salvation lies in being just, fair, impartial and in being a perfect steward of God's gifts.

Whoever misuses religion by using it to take advantage of people's faith in order to accomplish personal aims dictated by the desires of their own domineering self should know that they are committing an absolutely unpardonable, deadly sin, a sin that has a special added dimension. Because this sin is unforgivable, that person will have no intercessor in the other world and will necessarily have to undergo their punishment. Those punishments are so incredibly diverse that they surpass the limits of our knowledge. Here is only one illustration: imagine that a soul has been frozen in place, unable to make the slightest movement, but still remaining totally lucid and aware. In addition to this state of complete paralysis it also suffers from a continual sensation of extreme suffocation which never stops, while it is always completely conscious of its condition. This soul, whose natural constitutive state is to be constantly in motion, is as it were imprisoned in the mineral state, petrified like a living stone at the very limit of death. Such people are in a state, according to the Qur'an, 'where they are neither dead nor living'.

II

RELIGION

What is faith? You have compared faith to a light, a ray of light connecting the heart to God.

Yes, light, that's good . . . Let's find a comparison to start with, and then a definition. The field of our mind, of our consciousness, is something you don't see, that seems obscure to you. But then a certain brightness comes into that obscurity, like the dawn, and gradually that light appears and causes the darkness to vanish. That shadowy consciousness is illuminated by something which is faith. Faith is light: the more faith you have, the brighter and more luminous you are within yourself. When you put your belief into practice (if that belief is true), that light increases. It will enable you to see your inner being more clearly, and gradually it will lead you toward true certainty. Only you can never see its Source, or what the Source is.

This is why we compare faith to the dawn. For people who have no belief, who've lost their faith, the field of their heart is dark, gloomy, cold, without any attraction towards God. So we have to find the light.

Faith is like a light radiating from God that warms the heart and draws it toward its Source. Those who have faith feel inwardly warm and are attracted toward their Origin by this force. But someone without faith feels overcome by a spiritual frigidity which leaves them without any attraction or desire for God. Their heart tries to warm itself with the burning and smoky fires of their animal dimension, and their desire and attraction are drawn to material things. In addition there are those who seek to warm and enlighten their hearts by means of artificial lights such as false religions, misguided esoteric sects, and things of that sort.

To summarize, faith is a ray of light flowing from the Creator that penetrates each creature's heart. If the creatures don't lose their aptitude to receive it, that light will penetrate them, illuminate and warm their heart, soften and comfort them, and give them the motivation to advance toward their Creator, while also serving as their guide.

If someone believes in God without having this light, is that also faith?

But what is God? You don't really know God. If you believe in God that's because this light has already penetrated your heart.

You could say He is a Being who governs everything.

No, you can't compare God with anything else. He's something you can't encompass with your imagination. Who can't be imagined. God is the Creator, sustainer and controller of what is possible and of what exists: the creature is guided toward Him by His light, but will never know His essential Nature.

But how can you communicate with this Reality that you can't imagine? You have to have some kind of image or representation . . .

Yes, but that representation is not this God Who is light. Rather, it is a sort of 'crystallized' God that you can imagine. The *mazharullâh* (the manifestation of God through a particular human being) is precisely the point through which you can reach the light. But even the *mazharullâh* conceals his light. He transforms himself so that we can conceive him in our imagination; and if he takes away his body, once again we're unable to imagine him. But once you've transcended the need to imagine God you no longer need to concentrate on a particular form. From that moment on you are moving in what is infinite, and that's better. We're more at home in the infinite than in what is limited.

Once you're in infinity, does this relation you have with God still continue forever?
Yes, precisely. You keep the relation, only in infinity. That is the following stage.

Before reaching that stage, are we idolaters?
That isn't idolatry. For the beginner on the path it's the right way to reach the spiritual treasure. You just follow that 'vein' of faith. It's like a lottery where you've drawn the winning number. That's my perception of it.

Before this stage of light, isn't there another stage we could also call faith, but which is a fainter, less distinct sensation?
In the beginning that perception is less distinct: it manifests itself as a sort of inner attraction. Stop and imagine: what is faith? You have faith in the existence of God. But where is that feeling located, where does it come from, what is its source?

It's God Himself who gives it.
Of course it's His light. It's His light that you feel in your heart, your soul, your consciousness. That is a very profound awareness. We can increase it and we can diminish it, but we can't create it for ourselves: it's God who must give it to us.

But giving is also a human quality, it's still an image. So what's behind this expression of God's 'giving' us this light?

Precisely, you don't know what this One is Who gives off this light. The sun is a creature; it radiates its light, but involuntarily. With God that is voluntary: He can give His light or He can withhold it. Either that light illuminates us and penetrates our heart; or else, if the house of our heart has become hard and impenetrable, the light can't enter there.

What's the difference between this stage of faith and certainty?

Let's say you hear some voices behind a wall. You suppose there's something behind it, but you aren't sure what it is: it could be a radio, people talking, or something of that sort. So as long as you don't go behind the wall and see for yourself you won't have real certainty . . . True certainty comes from seeing for yourself the consequences of the actions you've carried out because of your authentic religious belief.

THE FOUNDATIONS OF THE AUTHENTIC RELIGIONS

When we speak of religion we mean those basic foundations and unchanging principles that are involved in the spiritual education of each human being's self until that person reaches perfection. Religion can only be truly understood by the spiritual senses. The more they are educated and awakened, the more our understanding of religion becomes clear, precise, and closer to the pure truth. And conversely, the less someone has worked at religion, the more they're controlled by the forces of their domineering self (the *nafs*) and the more their spiritual senses are weakened and become vague, imprecise and distant from the truth. They can even sink to such a state that they're no longer able to grasp the truth: then they become lost in the labyrinth of the different religions created by men, in the endless interpretations and

philosophical speculations which are not based on either
religious practice or real spiritual experience, and so they
lose their way.

The three principles of authentic religion are the unicity
of God, the eternity of the soul, and the existence of the
other world.

The Unicity of God

To know God means to come to be a true monotheist on the
basis of your own personal experience. You must come to
know God as the prophets, saints and true monotheists have
known Him. That means preferring God to everything else
– pleasure and wealth, power and prestige, family and
friends, even life itself. It means having God continually
present with you and relying only on Him: in short, becoming a lover and servant of God, and of Him alone.

If someone venerates a prophet, a saint or an authentic
Master, they shouldn't do so on account of that person, but
only for the sake of the reflection of the divine Essence that
appears through them. (Sometimes that Essence may even
be reflected by a mineral, a plant or an animal.) What one
worships is the divine Essence, not Its particular place of
manifestation. The beings who reflect that Essence can
change and disappear from our sight, but the divine Essence
always exists. So we must seek It and find It.

The person who aspires to this state can go far beyond
formalism and religious rituals. Although that person carries
out the rites of their religion, the exoteric dimension of the
different religions and their rites are not everything for
them; those things only constitute the first stage. Once the
thread of the heart has become connected to the divine
Centre, north or south, up or down, standing or seated –
none of these matter any more: everything that person says
is a prayer, everything they do is an act of worship that is
recorded in heaven, and they no longer have to repeat any

particular formula unless they want to. The story is told that the Buddah practised ascetic techniques for seven years and that eventually, having failed to obtain any result, he completely rejected all methods and rituals. But finally, one night while he was seated under a tree, the thread of his heart was united with the divine Centre and he understood whatever he wanted.

The Eternity of the Soul

The human being, who never dies, must understand this matter which is absolutely fundamental for each of us: our body is only a garment or receptacle for the true self, which is our angelic soul. It is the angelic soul that is the source of our power of choice, discernment, understanding, moral principles, the higher forms of creation, and many other things. The soul, or the true self, does not die with the body, and its life continues eternally unless it makes itself unworthy. Once it has left behind its bodily garment it keeps with itself all the powers of its senses, but now in a form that is more powerful, more precise and more sensitive than when it was bound to the body; and it will exist forever in the other world, which is its home from then on.

Just as everything in this world where we are living is subject to laws and a regular discipline that we have to take into account, so spiritual matters are likewise governed by strict and precise rules and laws. The slightest offence or violation, the smallest transgression we commit here, is seen and recorded, sometimes with serious consequences. Unfortunately for many people, we only possess in the other world what we have sown and come to deserve in this world. Whether or not someone happens to believe in the divine laws and the eternity of the soul, they will still have to bear the consequences of those actions in the other world; some of those consequences are eternal, and no one will be able to help them.

The Existence of the Other World and the Judgement

It is pointless to believe in the existence of the other world and then to talk about it like somewhere that doesn't concern us now. On the contrary, every person ought to become profoundly aware of the fact that the other world really does exist and that it directly concerns us, since we'll necessarily have to go there to be judged and to dwell there for all eternity.

To come to understand this question you need the help of an authentic, experienced Master or spiritual guide so that you can undertake the combat against your domineering self and put authentic spiritual teachings into practice in order to purify your self and awaken your spiritual senses. In this way you'll eventually come into communication with the other world to such a degree that you can clearly see and feel that that world does exist, and that each of us is inevitably destined to go there one day. You will notice the different levels of souls, and you'll see that the prophets and saints told the truth. You will see how bad people, evildoers and especially religious charlatans and pretenders live in a condition of spiritual agony and remorse, and also how good people, those who acted in accordance with their conscience, who have believed in and practised a true religion, live there in a state of happiness and bliss.

EXOTERICISM

The process of perfection involves every creature and it takes place in gradual stages. Religion is also created by God, and it is made up of four stages: exotericism, and the three stages of spirituality or 'esotericism' (*tarîqat, ma'rifat* and *haqîqat*). *Tarîqat*: you are looking for the way; *ma'rifat*: you know the way; *haqîqat*: you have reached the goal. Authentic exotericism constitutes the foundation and seed-bed for the perfection of religion. It involves both dimensions of the human being. Its spiritual dimension consists in believing in the fundamental principles of religion: the Unicity of God, prophecy, the eternity of the soul, and resurrection. Its psychic and bodily dimension is connected with the acts of worship and devotion, precepts for behaviour, social relations, and the like.

History shows us that human ways of thinking do advance with time and that as a result the needs of people's psychic and bodily dimensions also vary. That is why God has caused the religions to be revealed one after the other, according to the particular human needs and capacities at each time and place. The spiritual dimensions of those religions is always the same, but their psychic and bodily dimension has evolved according to the development of humankind. For example the exoteric aspect of Judaism stressed the first, psychic and bodily aspect of religion; while Christian exotericism tended to develop the second dimension; and the exotericism of Islam established a balance between those two aspects.

Each human being has two dimensions: our heavenly, angelic side, by its very nature, is full of love for God, and it is intrinsically concerned with the other world. Our second, psychic and bodily, dimension derives from our animal nature, and its concerns are directed toward material problems. The combination of these two dimensions forms each person's 'self'. An authentic religious exotericism expresses our duties toward God, toward our self, and toward others. Its impressions initially affect our psychic and mental level: that is the stage of formal, external knowledge. In order to gain a deeper understanding of the spiritual truths contained in the precepts of an authentic exotericism, a person has to enter those esoteric, spiritual stages that make up the level of the angelic soul.

Now what we are saying here concerns the authentic exotericism that was taught and practised by each of the prophets and their immediate disciples. It is through actually putting that exotericism into practice for ourselves that we can reach a real understanding of our duties. As for the exotericisms of our own time, they've taken on the colouring of men: they're more concerned with satisfying other people than with satisfying God. And often their deeds don't match up with what they preach. History shows us that they frequently take their false interpretations of religion to be immutable truths and then try to force their followers to accept those ideas: for example, the belief that the earth stands motionless at the centre of the universe, based on a mistaken interpretation of the Bible, or the condemnation of the notion of successive lives (after the fourth century). And there are many other examples, which have often resulted in acts of persecution.

What does it mean to have a shari'at?[1]

An authentic *shari'at* is the foundation and seed-bed for the esoteric dimension of religion. Its fundamental principles and its moral and religious precepts are a compass for all those who are seeking the pole of Truth.

If you're a Catholic, should you obey the Pope?

As for the rules concerning the bodily and psychic side of things, obey the Pope; but for the esoteric dimension you must have an authentic, experienced spiritual Master. Where esotericism and spirituality are concerned, the teachings of a spiritual Master who is Catholic should reflect the teachings of Christ.

The moral law flows from the divine law. A morality which doesn't flow from religion is a purely conventional morality, and that has no spiritual value for us.

If you follow the *shari'at* of a true, authentic religion you ought to observe the laws set forth and practised by the prophets, the saints and the leaders of those who practise that religion. Or else choose the *shari'at* following that one. For example, if you don't know whether or not you should have an abortion, you follow their orders, and then you are covered: if their orders were mistaken they are the ones who

are responsible. Or take another example: someone who is a
Muslim wants to eat a particular kind of meat and doesn't
know whether it's religiously permitted or not; if they refer
the decision to one of their religious authorities then they're
covered. However if you do become certain that a command given by a particular exoteric religious authority is
based on a false interpretation, then it's not in your spiritual
interest to follow that order, since by definition you can
only reach the Truth by practising what is true.

In the other world, you have to be registered in a particular *sharī'at*. In this spiritual school you have to have a *sharī'at*;
that is a basic prerequisite. Things that are forbidden in this
school, such as alcohol and pork, are forbidden for every
disciple, whatever their *sharī'at*. But you have to have a
spiritual identification, a *sharī'at*, to begin with.

Because someone loves Jesus doesn't necessarily mean
they are in the *shar'iat* of Jesus. I myself have a great vene-
ration for Jesus. If you leave the Christian *sharī'at* for Islam,
that doesn't mean you've left Jesus!

*Doesn't the act of moving from one prophet to another create
problems? Isn't it a sort of betrayal?*

The prophets are God's servants whom He has sent to
announce His commandments and principles to people and
to guide them towards Him. If the prophets considered
themselves the owners of their disciples that would be a
contradiction with what they have revealed. This question
comes from the undeveloped state of your spiritual concep-
tions about the religion of the prophets. Once the prophets
have completed their mission they rejoin their Beloved, and
they make up a single great, united family. The people of
faith in the different religions don't belong to the prophets
in the sense that there could be any sharing or betrayal or the
like: they belong to God. One more thing: haven't you ever
considered the possibility that several saints and prophets
might be one and the same spiritual personality, who carried
out those missions at different times?

Does this mean we have to know perfectly the sharî'at of our religion?

Everyone should know the rites of their sharî'at to the extent of what is possible for them; whenever a problem arises concerning its exoteric aspect they should consult a religious authority.

Each religion complements and supplements the preceding religion. To change religion, in this sense, is to pass through another spiritual stage. What this means is that the followers of the more recent religion have gained the possibility of advancing spiritually more effectively if they practise that religion as it was in the beginning. Even if a person changes their religion in this direction as a formality, that is still an advance unless they did so insincerely. Of course I'm not talking about the different religions of men, but the religion of Moses, of Christ, of Muhammad and of Ali. In the books of Moses there is relatively little discussion of spirituality. But the Gospels, on the other hand, speak only of spirituality and the esoteric dimension of religion; there is very little exotericism. In Islam, especially in true Shiism, there is a proper balance between exotericism and esotericism.

What religion will a soul be placed in during its next life?

Perhaps it won't come back here; but if it has to come back that will depend on what it has understood, acquired and accomplished.

Sometimes people hesitate about which sharî'at to choose.

They shouldn't stay in a state of indecision. You have to open your eyes and look, without any prejudice: God always shows the way to the person who prays sincerely for His help.

When you look at the situation of the different religions today, how could somebody think that it is good, for example, to move from Christianity to Islam?

I'm speaking about the religion of the prophets . . . Each religion completes and supplements the preceding one.

The principles of Christianity are very attractive – or rather the principles of Christ, his words.

Can one mix religion and politics?
According to our Master, you shouldn't get caught up in politics. Political activity and spirituality neutralize one another. You have to be in one camp or the other; you can't be in both at the same time.

But wasn't the Prophet of Islam involved in politics?
No he wasn't; or else we have to define what you mean by politics. If by politics you mean establishing social justice, then yes, Muhammad did use political means to establish social justice, without deviating from the straight path. But when politics leads you to become involved in lying and injustice . . .

As for the Prophet's various struggles, that's something entirely different: the enemies of the first Muslims wanted to annihilate them, so they were forced to defend themselves in order to survive. All the battles the Prophet fought were defensive, not offensive. The holy war has always been one of defence against an attack.

But the conquests of Islam weren't defensive . . .
That was after Muhammad; they were undertaken by Umar, the second caliph.

Did Jesus' twelve disciples, who are called saints, reach perfection?
In the beginning they hadn't reached perfection, since they denied Jesus. But after they underwent their martyrdom, only God knows.

It is said that Mary became the Vali[2] of her time, after Jesus.
That's possible, but I don't know.

When did Jesus begin his teaching?
When he was still in the cradle, he spoke with his mother.

People have written that Jesus didn't work for a living.
How do you know? Who wrote that? God doesn't allow His prophets to live at the expense of others.

What do you mean by 'safeguarding life as a precious trust'?
That you shouldn't voluntarily run the risk of dangers you can avoid. That you shouldn't commit suicide, either all at once or gradually. God has entrusted us with this life. Yes, we should be courageous, but we don't have the right to risk our life unless God orders us to do so.

So did Christ receive an order to go to the very end?
Yes, certainly.

Why did Imam Husayn defend himself at Kerbala?[3]
He didn't receive the order to let himself be killed, so he defended himself; he even wanted to leave. Husayn was also in that state where he had seen God and felt God, but since he hadn't received the order to become a martyr he defended himself; he didn't want to become a martyr because it was his wish, but because it was God's . . . There are certain moments when you are in such a state that you really do want to leave this earth. But Imam Husayn was able to control himself. He was determined, and he waited for God's command; he didn't give in to his own inclinations. He didn't hurry, and he waited until the third day. Otherwise he could have gone to his martyrdom on the first day, but he waited until the third.

If you are killed because of a command from God or because you follow the order of a divine person, that counts as a genuine martyrdom. But if there is no divine command or no order from a divine person, then it isn't real martyrdom. God always makes known those whom He has chosen. There are so many signs revealing the spiritual personality of a divine person that if you pay attention you can tell whether someone is truly a divine person or only a pretender.

The Christian martyrs died for Christ, who was a divine person. In Christianity, unlike Islam, a person doesn't have the right to conceal their faith in a situation where their life depends on it (*taqîya*). Since those Christians couldn't practise *taqîya*, and since they were killed for God's sake, they are true martyrs. But a Muslim must receive that order from the *Valî* of his or her time, and must be absolutely sure about that order.

When Jesus reappears, will people realize that his essence is on earth?

They won't realize it in the sense that people ordinarily imagine, but they will feel its beneficent effects . . . That's the way it is. If Christ reappears, a certain number of people will recognize him, and they will become the earth's representatives. These will be individuals who have reached a higher spiritual stage, who can profit from his spiritual teachings and who will recognize the person who has 'reappeared'. The number of such people depends on God.

But as for the others, those who haven't reached the stage where they can directly benefit spiritually from his person, they will still have the material and even the spiritual advantages of his presence. The spiritual advantage will be the strengthening of their faith, a greater attraction for spiritual rather than material things. Those who were attracted by the material world before Christ's reappearance will begin to ask themselves what's the use of running after so many material things, why shouldn't they also be working for their spiritual welfare, and so on. These ideas will just come to them, and the spiritual atmosphere of the earth will become predominantly positive.

Is it really recommended to go to church and other religious gatherings?

It is beneficial to go to church, to attend spiritual gatherings. Prayer in a group has its own specific advantage for the soul, and so does the place of prayer. Such gatherings are beneficial as long as their aim is divine and spiritual; otherwise they are harmful.

One sees people who follow Jesus' commandments, but who still don't reach their perfection.
When people apply Christ's laws they don't remain in a state of moderation; they tend towards one extreme or the other. That's because Jesus gave his lessons for advanced disciples, those at the high school level, not for the elementary classes where we are. Those persons you mention haven't reached the stage where they can assimilate and fully realize Christ's laws. When Jesus says, for example, 'if someone strikes you on the cheek, turn the other cheek', that's something a person can only do at the stage of complete surrender to God. But someone who is still in the stage of following their own will can't assimilate that teaching; it's still too early for them. That's why Islam also gives lessons for most ordinary people.

But there are also saints among the Christians?
Of course. There have been a great many genuine saints among them. But there are also some who weren't saints but who've been presented as such; be very careful not to fall into that trap. The religions of men have replaced the religions of the prophets, and that has happened everywhere, from Zoroaster down to Muhammad, although to different degrees. Present-day Buddhism may have relatively little to do with the Buddha. The Buddha is truly a prophet, and his religion was an authentic one. Zoroaster was also an authentic prophet, but how much of his teaching remains today? Here I'm speaking about opinions in general, not certain individuals.

Why have some holy scriptures been lost?

The people of those ages weren't worthy of them. They'd gone so far astray from the right path that they didn't deserve to have those scriptures in their possession. So God preferred for them either to be lost or else to be preserved in the hands of the saints and His prophets.

There are a great many discussions about particular religious prescriptions. For example, what are the sins for which Christians are responsible?

Christians, like Muslims, are responsible for those things which their religion considers to be sinful. If they do things contrary to the commandments given by Moses and by Christ, those actions are counted among their sins. In Islam, for example, you're told that alcohol is illicit, so drinking alcohol is a sin for Muslims. But the religion of Christians and Jews doesn't consider that a sin, so drinking alcohol isn't a sin for them.

In your book [The Path of Perfection] *you've written that the people of our age no longer see any need to believe in the One God in order to lead their lives. If they try to live according to their conscience, will they be unhappy in the other world?*

No, because if they truly continue to follow and abide by their conscience they will be guided toward God. When we say 'God' in this case that it not just a manner of speaking: the voice of conscience is the divine path. However, I see very few individuals who really do rely on their conscience. And in addition, if a person's conscience is not reinforced by faith in the final Judgement, it is a fragile support. The conscience by itself can easily waver.

Can we distinguish between the moral conscience (due to our education, social environment, and the like) and the spiritual conscience which comes from the soul?

The moral sense arises from the angelic soul, so it has its source in spirituality and is one of its aspects. Morality and conscience without religion are like a body without a head.

If we rely on morality alone that isn't enought; but if we take spirituality as our foundation, then we'll have morality as well. Our angelic soul adores God; therefore it is already religious. Morality is included in every authentic religion, or else we wouldn't be able to speak of the moral dimension of conscience.

The origin of this error is in those 'religions of men' which have focused their efforts on material and social problems, thereby neglecting our spiritual dimension. They act as though the prophets had come only in order to provide for people's material well-being in this world, not to save their spiritual life. There are societies without religion that have been able to provide their members with peace and order by observing the moral law; but they won't be able to suppress people's religious motivation. We ought to ask just where those societies found their moral laws. Of course every social group can also have its own 'morality': criminals, savages and the like all have their own moral code – but that is not the morality we all respect, which is derived from religion. So those societies have chosen moral laws of a religious origin while neglecting their Source. But is it logical to find our well-being in moral laws of religious origin while at the same time neglecting or rejecting religion itself? Or to believe in the authenticity of religion while at the same time saying that it was only made up by certain people? The contradiction is obvious.

Ever since Adam, those in power have tried everything they could to eliminate the idea of religion from people's minds. But they've never succeeded and they never will, because the heavenly part of each human being is by nature full of love for our Creator. The Buddha was only a single individual without worldly power. Christ was likewise only a man of the people, without any worldly authority, and with only a handful of disciples. But today they have more than a billion followers, while there's no trace at all of the most powerful figures of their time. With a little thought and reflection we can conclude that religion is not invented by men, but rather something that is given to people from above. The things created by men don't last for long; often they disappear without leaving a trace. People have acquired a sort of allergy to certain phrases endlessly repeated by official religious leaders who themselves fail to put those sayings into practice and who aren't very encouraging examples for those who do believe. That's why many people believe in spirituality and act according to the moral laws and their conscience, but don't want to hear about God. They're religious in their hearts, although they flee talk about God.

Since our own will is the cause of our suffering and unhappiness, what can we do to avoid that?

In order to avoid that we must follow our conscience, but our conscience as educated by authentic religious or moral laws and principles. Even if you don't want to follow a saint or a religion, you should at least follow the voice of your conscience. But which conscience? One whose laws are drawn from true religion.

Some people ask God each day to help us do His Will.

Yes, we ought to ask Him every day; that's correct. But that requires certain conditions. Except for exceptional cases like the saints, prophets and the like, you shouldn't expect God to shout in your ear 'You made a mistake!' whenever you do something wrong. God will guide us with means that are already here on earth. For example, you may want to travel somewhere by a certain road, but you notice that the police have stopped people from going that way for an hour or two. You shouldn't try to do everything you can to change your route in order to get where you're going, because that could well be a divine sign meant to save you from some danger. You have to pay attention: God sends messages to us through other people or other earthly means. Take another example: you find a job you like and they're ready to hire you, but then you lose it at the last minute. If you've already entrusted the decision to God you shouldn't be saddened by the eventual outcome. You should pay attention to these messages, these signs, while being careful not to become superstitious.

In addition, you should at least intend to practise the divine precepts, so that your request will have a certain credence with God; then He will guide you. If people don't create a certain right for themselves through their own efforts, then God has no special responsibility toward them. It is said: 'Knock, and it will be opened for you.' But as long as you haven't actually begun to practise the divine precepts, don't expect the door to be opened for you.

How should we make offerings?

It is an excellent thing to participate in acts of charity. Each person can make offerings and perform acts of charity according to the exotericism of their religion.

What is the place of music in spirituality?

Some of our prayers (*zikrs*) are accompanied by melodies, because the angelic soul loves music. The story is told that when God created Adam's body it remained without an angelic soul for a long time, because Adam's soul was disgusted by the body and didn't want to enter it. Then a group of archangels went inside it and began to play some heavenly music. And so Adam's soul, as soon as it heard that music, immediately entered his body . . .

Music is a divine creation; it is also a language, but a language more beautiful and sweeter than any speech. The power and profundity of music's effect on each being is directly proportional to that creature's degree of purity. The purest part of each being is its soul, and every creature with a soul is sensitive to music.

Just as language has its letters, so music is made up of notes, and innumerable compositions can be created through the arrangement of those notes. Each musical sound

— like every other creature — has its own specific qualities and characteristics, but its effects differ according to the listeners. Those effects depend on several different factors:

- The original nature of the listener's soul, as well as their physical and mental state, the education they've acquired, and so forth.
- The particular time and place.
- The listener's education, habits and social surroundings, the type of music that that person likes, as well as their inner intention and whether they're governed by their angelic soul or by their *nafs*. For example, some people listening to the very same music may want to dance and feel a nostalgic desire for past pleasures, while others may be filled with a deep sense of spiritual longing or an aching sadness for those dear to them who are now dead or far away. And other persons may feel a state of lightness and joy. In listening to the sacred music of Africans, for example, some people experience only a purely bodily pleasure.
- The person who created the music and those who perform it. A musician who possesses a certain spiritual force can cause his listener to experience whatever effect he wants. This factor controls all the others.
- Sometimes the effect depends on the music itself. Thus physicians in ancient times used special melodies for medical purposes. It's said, for example, that certain melodies are in harmony with the sounds of heaven, or that certain intervals can create a celestial harmony. This is where the higher souls come into play. The listener has only to ascend on the wings of this music and fly through heaven. But if the person playing the instrument has sufficient spiritual force they don't simply follow the melody of the instrument; rather it's the musician who carries the music along with himself.
- The instrument, or whatever the source of the musical sound may be. For example, those other musical sources can be the voices of animals, the sound of the wind or

other natural phenomena (whether those are ordinarily audible or not to the unaided ear), and the sounds of the metaphysical world for those who are spiritually awakened. Those sounds can have a material origin (as with the voices of minerals and plants praising their Creator), or their source may be purely spiritual (such as the voices of invisible beings). We have both a physical ear and an ear of the soul, and each of them was created to hear a part of all these sounds and voices.

● Sometimes the instrument itself has a particular power which it was given by a spiritual authority. For example, we know of a horn that causes death in the direction it is blown (no matter who happens to play it), or a lute (*tanbûr*)[4] that transmits heavenly melodies whenever someone plays it.

Scientists conceive of God as a form of energy. Is that idea correct?

Energy is one of the manifestations of God, but energy itself does not think, does not order things or direct them toward particular ends. Nor have they been able to prove that energy created itself. The more science advances, the more people will believe in the necessity of the existence of an original point of creation, a primordial Cause.

What does it mean to ask God for something?

Not everyone knows how to ask for God's help, because the verbal formula by itself isn't always enough. These are conditions for an effective request. Someone who fulfils their duties toward God acquires a certain right: if you manage to observe the divine precepts, and if your wholehearted intention is to obey God, then your request will be accepted. But if you don't put the divine precepts into practice, or if you don't even know what they are, then of course you shouldn't expect that your request will automatically be accepted; because anybody can make purely verbal requests.

God Himself doesn't need any intermediary, but who could have the capacity and ability to withstand direct contact with Him? That's why the world we live in is the world of cause and effect; nothing happens here without cause and effect. When God wishes to contact human beings, there has to be an intermediary. Even if He Himself contacted someone, that person would be disoriented. Moses didn't understand at first: he saw a light talking to him, and even then it was through the intermediary of a burning bush that God spoke to him.

Can we discover God in ourself?

You don't know what God is; you don't really know him. But there is a particle of God within us. And by becoming aware of that particle, by coming to know it, you can come to know how God is.

God is lovable and detestable . . . We are like children: we want to have God completely for ourselves. When we see that He is equally good with everybody we can't stand it. In Ali's battle against Mu'awiya, Ali's enemies had begun by occupying the well and keeping his forces from having any water. But later, when Ali's forces had driven away their enemies, he ordered his soldiers to let their opponents have some of the water. That was something many of his supporters hated because they couldn't understand that Ali only acted according to God's will. God does the same thing. Many of those soldiers couldn't stand His justice, and so they abandoned Ali. But those who had reached the point of really knowing Ali didn't abandon him, and they understood that he had to act that way.

Feeling God's effects in yourself is not the same as actually seeing God in yourself. Then you actually see that you are God, that everything is God. When you begin to see God in yourself you see Him everywhere. If you have the eye to see God, you see Him everywhere. That's a particular sensation, an awareness you can't define.

You've written that God answers each of us and knows each person's state.

The domineering self can influence the angelic soul and make it so sick and weak that a person can no longer perceive God's signs. His answer to each individual depends on that person's spiritual state, their nearness to or distance from God, and also their particular constitution.

You write: 'It is possible to reach a point where nothing more separates the soul from God, where the person only sees Him.' Is that the state of a saint?

That's the state of someone who has reached perfection. That state can happen to someone temporarily during the course of the path of perfection, but when that person reaches perfection it becomes permanent: that is absolute Love.

Which form of prayer is most important for God?

I think the best prayer is to actually put into practice the divine precepts. To always have God with you, right in front of your eyes, to feel that He is always with you, not to feel alone.

But some people are afraid of God; they feel as though God could be watching and criticizing them.

The fear of God is really a fear of yourself, like a lover who is afraid of displeasing his beloved because of his behaviour. Mothers, who didn't even create their children, love and adore them and carefully watch over them; so how could you imagine that the watchful oversight of our God, Who created us, could be any different? God's watching over us is that 'divine Regard' we've already discussed.[5] This indicates such people haven't yet experienced the ineffable joy of feeling God.

What about those who haven't reached that state: what precept should they follow?

They must follow the covenant made with God at their creation. Then your prayer corresponds to the state you're in.

Is it all right to pray with mental words?

That is the mental, psychic state of spirituality. You have to strive to reach the spiritual state of prayer. God doesn't expect any other prayers but those that are appropriate to the particular stage of each individual. If a person is at the mental stage their prayers will also be mental, and God accepts them as such.

After each of his prayer sessions the Master would say the following prayer:

Wash me clean of every sin, every trespass, every misdeed.
In your Majesty, cast a glance at your slave.
In your Loving Mercy, give a shelter to this dog.
My Creator, forgive me, forgive my father and mother,
and all the men and women of faith;
Brighten our hearts with the light of faith;
Illuminate our vision with the light of Ali.[6]

Is there a special form or path to worship God?

Each person worships God in their own way.

III

THE SELF

You've said that we must apply the precepts of religion, put them into practice, and not aim at anything else. What are those precepts?

Study the principles of the path of perfection and apply them in practice, to the extent you've understood them. Essentially what we must do is to fight against the domineering self (the *nafs*).

Spiritual methods depend on the exoteric aspect of religion, and according to you they change according to the particular time, place, intellectual level and civilization. What is the method appropriate to our own time?

Some people weaken their bodies with the aim of strengthening their souls. That method is mistaken, and it is the opposite of our own: it's by developing the angelic soul that you come to control the domineering self. Most of the methods that are prevalent today only serve to weaken the domineering self, but they don't develop the soul. Of course when such individuals weaken the body or the *nafs* (the complex of psychic manifestations arising from the body) they do come into contact with their soul. It's like the two pans of a pair of scales: if you take away the weight of the *nafs*, the angelic soul rises. But that soul hasn't become any more developed as a result. When you weaken the *nafs* you've committed a sin and you haven't perfected the soul. Therefore the right method consists in strengthening the body and the *nafs* while fortifying the soul even more, so that it can control them. For only a strong and healthy soul can reach perfection.

The *nafs*, or domineering self, is the whole complex of instincts arising from the body. It carries out its duty, and the soul also fulfils its duty. The *nafs* knows no limit to its desires; it is like an infant. The angelic soul must come to govern, moderate and control it. On the other hand the soul cannot advance at all without the *nafs*; it's only with the help of the *nafs* that it can acquire the potential of moving toward its perfection.

What are our psycho-spiritual needs?

There are the needs of the soul and those of the body. With regard to the needs of the body, you should treat it exactly as though you were an animal: you should feed it, safeguard its well-being, make it strong, and give it everything it needs to preserve its health.

Since those two forces are combined in each human being, there are certain mixed needs. The more the animal side dominates, the more your needs are weighted down with animality; the more the side of the angelic soul is in control, the more your needs are drawn toward spirituality and the more your desires are in harmony with the divine precepts. For example, take a man who is married and earning a good living: if his animal needs are controlling him he can't be satisfied with a single woman; he wants other women, all the money in the world, all the power in the world, because his animal side drives him to excess in these things. If he were actually a pure animal he wouldn't behave like that, because once the bodily needs of animals are satisfied they simply sleep and don't desire anything more.

The *nafs* is made up of those animal characteristics whose purpose is to sustain our life as a human-animal. The qualities of the non-dangerous animals include our desires to sleep, eat, reproduce, and so forth, while the attributes of the

harmful animals in human beings make up that 'domineering self' which we have to fight. Those are the all–consum-
ing, destructive, aggressive characteristics.

Aren't education and social surroundings just as important as the
angelic soul in forming a person's psyche?
The Master mentioned seven factors that influence each
person's individual constitution:
1. The particular hereditary factors from their father and
   mother.
2. The composite hereditary factors of the blood-line from
   the preceding three generations of ancestors, including
   the parents.
3. The state of mind of both parents at the moment of
   conception.
4. The effects of the food that person eats.
5. The effects of the specific time and place.
6. The effects of their upbringing and family situation.
7. The effect of the divine Will, for those who deserve it,
   according to the specific aptitude they were created with.
   That's why God assigned one of His archangels as a
   servant of the Truth and as an intercessor for the creatures, in order to support the angelic soul against the
   domineering self.
One of the factors favouring the attraction of the divine
Will to a particular individual is that person's good actions
in their preceding lives. Why did God wish for this soul to
come back in favourable surroundings and for that soul to
fall into an unfavourable *milieu*? For example, one person
may find himself in a setting where people talk of nothing
but God, while another finds himself in a situation where
there is nothing but blasphemy: if that person becomes an
unbeliever, then of course that's because of their surroundings. We have to ask ourselves what that person did during
their preceding lives in order to deserve such a situation. But
what about those people who have had a materialistic, atheist education and who still become believers? That can't be

explained simply by the psychic influence of their environment. The divine Will is more significant than all those other factors, and It only affects those who deserve it.

What is the nature of the struggle against the nafs?
It is the ongoing, continuous and unending inner work, throughout our life, of controlling the desires, wishes and demands of our domineering self and keeping it from exceeding the limits set by God.

You have advised using mental self-suggestion to fight the nafs.
For example, if you have a quick-tempered disposition, begin by telling yourself that anger is very bad for both the mind and the body and that it is condemned by all the religions, as well as by society. Continue to repeat that to yourself all the time, and then set up a programme to fight that weak point. The first time you become angry you won't be able to avoid it. But you should try to recognize what role your own will plays in that process; your will can keep you from showing that anger, from acting it out. So after a while the outward aspect of your anger will become more internalized, even though the anger itself doesn't change. In the next stage you'll begin to notice that your anger is even becoming weaker within you. Then you won't become angry at all. And in the final, highest stage you can make yourself appear angry in your voice and bodily attitude without having any anger at all in your heart. You aren't angry, but you can play that role, like an actor or like parents who are educating their child and want the infant to think they're angry. That's the stage when you've truly overcome that weak point.

Some people try to control their nafs for purely psychic, rather than spiritual ends.
To begin with, it is preferable to control yourself and not to act out your passions. But if someone does what I've described for a purely psychic purpose, without any refer-

ence to the path of spiritual perfection, they will be unhappy and run the risk of simply repressing the problem and having other complexes; the outcome will necessarily be unstable. However if someone does that for God's sake the results will be the opposite, because the divine factor in the psyche creates a sort of spiritual 'antibody'. If someone who is fighting against their anger receives divine help, then an anti-anger substance will appear in their psyche and that person will permanently overcome their anger without that giving rise to inhibitions and other complexes. But if they leave out that divine, spiritual element the psychic immunity won't be permanent and they run the danger of creating new complexes and repressions.

If this process of self-suggestion isn't carried out for a divine purpose (for example, if it's done under the orders of a psychiatrist or of a false master) the results will be fragile and unstable. But if the self-suggestion takes place in a divine path, under the orders of an authentic spiritual Master, the aim of the suggestion will become a permanent character trait of that individual and the process won't lead to any unfortunate consequences, repressions or complexes.

There are several ways to fight the nafs. It's been said that when a person becomes detached, the domineering self automatically submits to their control. Isn't it really the opposite of that: it's when you have fought the domineering self that you become detached?

You need God's help to fight against the domineering self. Otherwise, as long as a person's desires are satisfied and they don't feel restricted they'll pretend to be unattached and contemptuous of those desires. But as soon as they try to restrict themselves in order to train themselves spiritually, or whenever their nafs can't fulfil one of its needs, then their nafs rebels and takes control.

What about the method that consists in not wanting anything, is that good?

Who said not to want anything? You can't do it. When you fight against the domineering self that characteristic grows and develops only gradually. It's the result of long years of continual work, of the progressive growth of your soul. It's a whole complex process, and all that has to come into being gradually. When your angelic soul grows, that characteristic is born in you and slowly takes form; it doesn't happen overnight. However self-suggestion does help a great deal in the beginning. In everything. We ourselves can perform the work required by this stage of self-suggestion, but we don't have any power over the heart's desires. We aren't the masters of our heart. What we can do is to begin to control our *will*. We can work on our will, and gradually our heart will also be corrected. So the first stage is self-suggestion. The second stage is based on personal experience, on trial and error. Sometimes you're the one who takes the initiative, and at other times it's God. Never forget to pray for God's help in all the stages of the struggle against the *nafs*, because it's impossible to control it without His help.

Are there any special methods for this process of self-suggestion?
We're actually doing that all the time. We don't have any artificial techniques: our method is in accordance with the precepts of religion, tradition and morality as our Master has taught them to us. The difference between our work and the approach of psychologists is that their results, because they don't work for the sake of God and the angelic soul, are often unstable or temporary, while what we obtain is permanent and lasting.

What is a 'weak spot'?
The *nafs* is a complex whole that includes both defects and weak spots. The definition of a weak spot is that you can't fight it with your own will and self-suggestion alone. If you do succeed in fighting a particular aspect of your *nafs*, then that isn't a weak point. I don't mean that you can't fight it at

all, but that you have a special weakness with regard to that point. With our other defects we still find it very hard, difficult to fight them. But with our weak spots we feel helpless. For example, this particular person is powerless against their anger; they struggle with it, but they're helpless. Only an authentic Master can help us overcome our weak spots. The trouble is, some people forget even to cry for help from their Master at those moments.

Each person has only a limited number of weak spots. When you fight your other defects you also strengthen yourself against your weak spots.

Is a weak spot the most hidden aspect of a person?

No, it's the most obvious, although it may be hidden from that person himself. But as you work on yourself a little you'll discover it.

To begin with, a weak spot is something you simply can't resist. You have to distinguish between weak spots and defects more generally: not all our defects are weak spots, but all weak spots are also defects.

Perfection is absolute balance and harmony in everything. Even a good moral attribute, if it is manifested to an excessive degree in someone, can become an imperfection. Everything that goes beyond the right balance and measure becomes a defect, or rather, you could say, a lack of perfection.

What is true for one spiritual stage is not valid for a different stage. There isn't any contradiction; it's just that things are said for different cases, different moments, different stages . . . Sometimes a Master is speaking of a general problem that applies to everyone, while at other times it involves a particular individual who asks a personal question and receives an answer that is apparently different from the general response.

How can we discover our weak spots?

Observe yourself: when there are certain things you're

completely unable to resist, that's a weak spot. For example, one person may have a weak spot for money: they can't resist the opportunity of picking up even a small amount of money wrongfully, and they're even less able to resist where a large amount is at stake. So that's their weak spot. But with other people that's not the case: you can offer them any amount of money and they're able to resist. Let's take some other examples. With men, the desire for power or sexual desire are the most obvious cases: some people are able to resist those desires while others are enslaved to them. With women it's things like jealousy, curiosity or the instinct of seduction that are more often apparent. Now everyone may have such desires; but it's when a person is helpless against them that they become weak spots.

When you're struggling against a weak spot and are unable to overcome it, at the moment you're about to give in you should cry out inwardly and ask your Master for help. Then you'll feel an extraordinary force and you'll be able to resist. But that doesn't mean this force will stay with you forever; it has only saved you from a dangerous situation. Once that crisis is over the weak spot will come back again; but your soul gradually becomes stronger as a result of these struggles, and it also becomes stronger when it encounters this weak spot.

For example, fear can be a weak spot. Everyone feels fear, but some people are completely paralysed by it; so that is a weak spot for them. (For example, the fear of losing something, fear of performing badly, and so on.) But in any case we have to act, and if we're sometimes mistaken that can't be helped. Spiritual matters are judged according to both our intentions and the way they are actually put into practice. If someone makes a mistake that is of little importance compared with the experience they have gained. Only experience can make God's support and direct influence immediately real for you: the more such experiences you have the more this feeling of God's presence with you will become real and the more your *tavakkul* (absolute trust and confidence in Him) will increase. It's through the experience of such tests and trials, and not by their words, that you can distinguish a true, divine Master from false masters. The stronger your trust in God becomes the less you'll be afraid.

Can doubt be a weak spot?

Doubt is more of a spiritual illness than it is a weak spot. As a rule, weak spots are natural instincts that have come to control us. But both doubt and pride are sicknesses of the soul, while the weak points are natural instincts in us. If you fail in your struggle against a weak spot that doesn't make your soul sick, but only keeps it from advancing. Weak spots create a barrier, an obstacle blocking your path.

There is also what we could call 'natural doubt', which forces a person to examine and clarify their problems more exactly and precisely. On the other hand, the spiritual sickness of doubt prevents people from becoming solidly established in their path and will eventually send them wandering astray.

You can obtain some improvement by struggling against an aspect of the nafs, but then as soon as you let go for a while you fall back almost to the same point where you started.

You have to start again and keep going, and little by little you will reach the point of controlling your *nafs*. Gradually the *nafs* will become weaker in relation to the soul. But you have to be vigilant all the time. When you're constantly struggling, sometimes you'll feel physical and psychic fatigue. You shouldn't let that get to you. If you have the possibility of changing your surroundings, of resting a while, there's no harm in that. But if not, those symptoms will still gradually go away. Bad health can slow people down and even stop them from advancing along the path, which is why it's our duty to take care of our bodily health and hygiene.

Poverty can also be an obstacle. At the beginning of the path it's preferable not to have either too much or not enough, but just what is necessary for a normal, moderate life. For example, if a student of this spiritual school happens to be in a state of need it's because they shouldn't have any more than that for the time being. If they did have any more they might lose their faith. There are some people who quickly forget about spirituality as soon as they become rich. God protects them by keeping them in difficult circumstances. Such individuals are especially common among simple, underprivileged folk who have to work very hard to earn their living. As soon as they become wealthy they forget God. Needless to say, such individuals haven't really understood the meaning of the path. They want spirituality as a sort of insurance for their material life: once they have no more material needs, they no longer feel any need for God either. So long as the soul of such individuals is weak it's better for them to have just enough to live on. However someone who has a strong soul can have great riches without that hindering their advancement toward perfection; wealth has no harmful effect on such a person. Everything depends on the particular individual.

Psychology teaches us that our true intentions are often hidden behind an outward, conscious intention. Given that fact, how can we be sure of our own good intentions where spirituality is concerned?

Psychologists can't judge the truthfulness and sincerity of a person's intentions; but God can judge them, and you too can judge whether your intentions are good or bad. The psychologist has to judge according to the visible evidence, and he can't know what someone's intention was at the moment of decision. Everything we do is recorded: God, or whoever is able to see a person's spiritual record, sees the truthfulness of the intention that has been set down there. A person can also be mistaken about their own intentions. Some people deceive themselves; they really know their intentions, but they try to fool themselves.

All of us are more or less caught up in fooling ourselves.

It's very difficult not to; you really have to work very hard and practise not deceiving yourself. That's because of the *nafs*; it's continually arguing with us in order to persuade and convince us. 'Fooling yourself' really means just that: letting yourself be convinced by your domineering self.

But at the same time you're fooling yourself you also know or sense that you're doing that.

When you begin to pay attention you'll gradually understand that you're fooling yourself. But if you don't pay attention you won't understand because you're so used to doing it. For example, in the case of people who follow false religions or false masters there is something telling them that that's not the truth: they're fooling themselves.

How do you categorize our thoughts?

I divide our thoughts as follows:

1. Wandering, random thoughts. These are wanderings, infantile imaginations, reveries without any basis in reality. The imagination roves along its own course, portraying all sorts of improbable and pleasing things: for example, that you have limitless powers, that you could do this or that, and so forth.

2. Ridiculous and ludicrous thoughts. These are the thoughts of a student of the spiritual path that leave that person open to ridicule, that allow certain groups of invisible spirits to make fun of them. For example, you may run away from a simple test, or fail or misunderstand it, because of a feeling of fear or a lack of faith. That can also happen on other occasions, not just during spiritual trials.

3. Negative thoughts, such as hatred, jealousy, and the like.

4. Poisonous thoughts, such as pride, spiritual doubt and uncertainty, and so on.

There are some psychic disturbances whose origin is unknown, which have no organic source, and others which are acquired in this life, such as the various complexes developed during childhood or due to the particular conditions of a person's life. All of these psychic illnesses, whether they are acquired here or have no organic source, can be healed with the methods of 'spiritual therapy' – that is, through spiritual treatment and working on the soul. One part of our work consists in that.

Is a psychic weakness the sign of a weakness in the soul?

No, that doesn't indicate a weakness of the soul, but it can have harmful consequences for the soul.

For example, a person may have a healthy soul imprisoned in a sick body. You know that the insane can be physically sound; it's their mental state that is defective. They can't make any progress on the spiritual path when they aren't even responsible for their worldly, civil affairs. From the divine point of view it's the same, because in principle the civil laws have their origin in the religious laws. The soul of such an individual is in prison throughout its life. On the other hand, if someone has certain innate, incurable psychic defects, that may also be a punishment for the soul. Such people have certain psychic characteristics that keep their soul from functioning normally.

What attitude should we have when we know that a specific psychic feature is innate and that there isn't any cure?

When the soul develops and becomes strong it can influence our psychic aspect . . . That particular feature may be diminished or it may not. Some psychic problems can be relieved by psychotherapeutic methods, while others aren't affected by that approach but can be cured by a spiritual treatment. However if the problem is a punishment, nothing will affect it as long as the punishment lasts. The origin of non-organic psychic disturbances is also sometimes influenced by extrinsic causes.

Is a healthy psyche usually associated with a strong nafs?

It's really the psyche that is important, not so much the body; because there have been saints who were invalids, but who were genuinely saints from every point of view. But on the other hand I've never seen someone insane become a saint. So when people speak of 'a sound mind in a sound body' that really refers to a healthy psyche.

Doesn't the one imply the other?
There is a relation between the two, but ordinarily the angelic soul should control the psychic, mental aspect, unless the soul has become sick or weakened for some special reason. A sick soul loses its strength. But if it hasn't lost its strength, then normally it keeps the psychic aspect under its control. An illness of the psychic, mental aspect cannot make the angelic soul sick. For example, a soul that is completely healthy and strong can carry a person ahead spiritually, even with a psychic illness. But the opposite is not true.

When the psyche is healthy, is the soul normally healthy too?
Not necessarily; an attraction toward true spirituality is one sign of a healthy soul.

Can the angelic soul influence the psyche?
The soul can influence the psyche, and in proportion to its strength it can influence and control illnesses of psychic origin. It can't affect organic diseases of the brain, but it can influence all the different forms of psychic disorders and mental imbalances whose origin is not organic. Psychology still doesn't understand very well the deeper causes of all these mental illnesses and tends instead to treat the symptoms. We maintain that a psychic illness of non-organic origin can even be cured by the power of the angelic soul.

There are two kinds of psychic illnesses: innate ones, and those which are acquired. In either case there may be an organic, bodily factor, or there may not be one. A person may have a small tumour in the brain and hear voices or have visions; those things will disappear once that tumour or lesion is removed.

Sometimes the cause is in ourselves, and sometimes it is outside of us, as in the case of certain harmful spirits. In that case psychiatrists can't do anything. I've compared the way those spirits work to the influence of germs: germs attack the body when its defences have been weakened and a path of entry appears. Those harmful spirits attack the psyche when a person's faith becomes weakened and disappears. People who have no faith are always at the mercy of these forces.

Some cases of hysteria are very similar to cases of possession.

Exactly. Some of them are caused that way, but we can't say that all cases of hysteria are like that.

In the past people used to say that insanity came about whenever someone was possessed by demons or *jinn*. Sometimes that is the case, but not always. A person's psychic sphere is possessed in such a case, but that psychic domain is under the control of the angelic soul, and the person's brain is a transmitter.

How can a possessed person be freed from the influence of the jinn?

In order to exorcize someone you have to have power over the *jinn*. So you need to be either a saint or a being who has been authorized to do this. It isn't even sufficient simply to be a saint: in order to command the spirit that possesses someone you must also have overcome the group of *jinn* to which that spirit belongs. For the *jinn* are also God's creatures, and they have their own process of perfection. That's why they can follow our prophets and saints. This is all totally different from magic. The magician is someone who has himself been conquered by the *jinn*: they only co-operate with him in order to lead him astray; by getting involved with them he has become their slave.

What is the cause of para-psychic phenomena such as ghosts, objects that move by themselves, and things like that?

We can't tell which spirits those may be; they could be human spirits or non-human ones. Every object has its own attractive force. The souls of people who have lived on earth also have their attractive force, and it's through the connection between these two kinds of forces that the souls of the dead can move objects and influence the thoughts of a living person.

Is there a lesson that should be drawn by those who've had this sort of experience?

There are signs from the invisible world intended to constitute a sort of ultimate argument (*itmâm hujjat*)[1] in the physical world. This kind of experience is an *itmâm hujjat* for those people who claim they've perceived nothing of the invisible, spiritual world and therefore don't believe in it. God sends them signs like these to see if they'll return.

Do the souls that contact the followers of spiritism have God's permission?

Without God's permission they wouldn't say anything. If they're the souls of human beings they don't lie, although you have to know how to distinguish and interpret what they say. But if they are the souls of other spirits, what they say may be true or false.

And what if a person has spiritual contacts with the souls of friends, for example?

They could also be distracting spirits, or derisive, mocking ones who have taken on the form of old friends. I strongly discourage the students of this Path from getting involved with spiritism.

Are spiritual love and carnal love incompatible?

Yes. Love is a more or less intense wave of attraction towards something, which is manifested by that desire and sentiment of devotion a person feels with regard to their beloved. Love is a positive attraction God has given as a special trust to each creature, an attraction that serves to motivate each creature to advance toward the Source of its perfection. That feeling remains pure in every earthly creature, except for human beings and ... But with human beings the purity of that sensation depends on each individual's psycho-spiritual state. A person who has been subjugated by their own domineering self, whose psycho-spiritual state is overwhelmed by the waves of the *nafs* and its helpers, loses that spiritual awareness and forgets that there could exist any love other than carnal love and the love for material success. In order to feel that divine Love we have to purify our psycho-spiritual state from the burning, suffocating waves and neutralizing forces of the domineering self. As long as we haven't undertaken that purification, divine Love doesn't exist for us.

Bodily love can also be divided into healthy and unhealthy loves. The healthy kind of love is that which God, through His religion, has permitted for people, such as the love of our parents and children and the love of our fellow human beings. To love your child, your spouse, health, exercise, travel, music, beneficial sciences: none of those things keeps someone from feeling God's Love. But that sort of 'love' which has its source in the domineering self is intemperate and illicit, such as the love of power, of wealth, of sensual lust and so forth. That love with its roots in the domineering self neutralizes spiritual Love.

When the angelic soul is in love, is that person's body also in love?

In certain cases one angelic soul may be in love with another angelic soul and there is a relation between those two persons: they feel an attraction toward one another, and if they haven't been educated about spirituality they may mistakenly translate that affinity as a sort of bodily desire. The great lovers like Tristan and Isolde, Romeo and Juliet, or Farhad and Shirin did not feel a carnal attraction; theirs was a true Love translated into a human passion. Or between Jesus and his disciples (both men and women), it was a purely spiritual Love.

For example, there are mystical poems that speak of Love: when a spiritual person reads them he immediately understands their profound inner meaning. But when the reader is someone submerged in their own bodily desires they interpret those same poems in terms of carnal human love, and you can't make them understand. It's the same as with faith: what can you give to someone who has destroyed their faith? You can't give them faith. It's God who gives faith. Faith is a particular sensation, an awareness: it's a light from God that penetrates and illuminates the heart. For those who've destroyed their faith it's as though their souls were dead: whatever divine influences they may see, whatever divine words they may hear, those things have no effect on them and fail to touch them.

And what about the body?

The body has been given to us by God so that we can use it to reach our goal of perfection. The body is indispensable for our soul's accomplishing its task of perfection; therefore we should respect it.

What is the significance of the so-called erotic poems in the Bible, such as the Song of Songs?

There are no adequate words to describe spiritual Love, so people use images of sensible things to explain it.

However we can't and shouldn't believe blindly in everything that is now in the Bible. I do believe unquestioningly and absolutely in the authentic sayings of prophets like Moses and Jesus, but we can't be sure that everything in the Bible is exactly what the prophets or saints said. In order to be sure you would have to do more research into the formation of the Bible.

Don't you think that bodily love is a way to get closer to someone you love?

There can be certain spiritual affinities between souls, and bodily love may bring them closer together, provided that there are no religious, moral and social prohibitions in their case; but if there are such restrictions they should be satisfied with that spiritual affinity. Bodily loves that aren't sustained by an affinity between souls are passing and ephemeral. People are born with the capacity for pure Love within them, but their imaginations are gradually influenced by false, misunderstood and erroneous ideas.

I don't deny that bodily attractions exist, but in my opinion there is no pure Love in such carnal attraction. Bodily 'love' is an excess of sexual desire; it isn't true, pure Love. Love is a spiritual reality. The word itself is truly a holy word, and we shouldn't misuse it by employing it to refer to the instincts of animals in a state of sexual deprivation. This same 'love' that exists between animals also exists in the bodily love of human beings. The sexual coupling of the human species is by itself an animal activity that doesn't go any further than our animality and doesn't last. If that sort of love goes on and becomes deeper, that's because it is sustained by an affinity between souls. True, genuine Love is unselfish, constant and pure.

There is a woman who feels a bodily desire for the Master each time she looks at his picture.

She has a pure soul, but she misinterprets her reaction under the influence of the education provided by her social *milieu*. If she advances a little in spirituality her state will change and her desire will become a spiritual Love. But if that idea persists she should watch out for the effect of negative influences.

Saint John of the Cross and Saint Teresa have written that their body thirsted for Christ. What does that mean?

That does have a meaning; it may mean that they feel a

longing to sacrifice their body for God, their Father. When Jesus said 'my Father', that was right.

You've written that the separation between the body and soul diminishes during the state of sleep.

That separation diminishes to the extent that the power of the body is decreased so that the angelic soul can more readily manifest itself in an individual. When a person is awake, the conscious communication between the soul and the body is disrupted because of the influence of the domineering self. The more that influence of the *nafs* decreases, the more you become conscious of your soul. Those individuals who've reached the point of completely controlling their domineering self, even when they are awake, can communicate perfectly with the metaphysical world.

Sleep is as it were a means of diminishing this power of the *nafs* that separates the angelic soul and the body. Let's take the example of an electrical current. Suppose that we block that current with an insulating medium, such as an insulating gas (assuming that exists). The greater the concentration of that insulator, the stronger the interruption of the current. Now you could say that the domineering self, when it is aroused, gives off a sort of 'smoke' that keeps the manifestations of the angelic soul from reaching our consciousness. On the other hand, when we are sleeping that *nafs* gives off less smoke. Spiritual dreams are an irrefutable sign of the existence of the angelic soul.

The domineering self arises from the body. The poor angelic soul is already intermingled with the impressions of the *basharic* soul, but at the same time the *nafs* also creates, so to speak, the source of this smoke: if an object is in the presence of those fumes it is saturated with that smell and retains it even if the smoke is no longer there. During your dreams, while you are in the state of sleep, you can see the soul although it still smells like that smoke; but when you're in the waking state this smoke is so thick you can't even see the soul. What the smoke of the domineering self comes from is animal life, the waking state, the body. When the body is in a state of sleep it gives off less smoke, and the person dreams. At that moment the consciousness that is dreaming is not so overwhelmed by the thickness of that smoke.

Animals dream of events from their animal life: eating, running, fighting, and things like that. In the human being, who is made up of the angelic soul and the animal soul, dreaming is a mixture of the two influences, and the type of dream depends on the relative preponderance of one or the other. If the domineering self predominates, then it is a merely psychic kind of dream: that person will go into the next world, after their death, in the same sort of state; they won't understand anything more. On the other hand, if the angelic soul predominates then in that case it will be a spiritual dream.

A spiritual dream leaves a deep and lasting impression. Its memory stays with you, and you have an inner feeling of confidence in the authenticity of what you have seen.

Sleep is a test of each person's spiritual state and of the influence of the domineering self: the more smoke or vapour there is – that is, the greater the power of a person's *nafs* – the less their angelic soul is able to ascend and the less it can manifest itself. In that case the individual's dreams are purely psychic, not spiritual. These are the sort of dreams that have been used by certain forms of psychology to support the claim that there is no soul and that dreams have a purely psychic, animal origin.

Is it possible to distinguish between dreams arising from the unconscious and spiritual dreams?

I've already spoken to you about the process of dreaming. Even animals dream. There are three basic categories of dreams: purely angelic, spiritual ones; purely *basharic*, animal ones; and a mixture of the first two types.

There are two nervous systems in human beings: the autonomic nervous system and the conscious, voluntary nervous system. The autonomic nervous system is ordinarily not under the control of our will, while the other nervous system is controlled by our will and has the power of discrimination. When someone has a pain in the abdomen they don't know just where it is, whether it is their stomach, liver or pancreas. They don't know. They only know that their abdomen hurts; that's all. It's said that each individual has a sort of 'vegetative' awareness of all that. Likewise the dreams of animals are vague and imprecise; as soon as they wake up it's over.

But we also have another nervous system that is voluntary and conscious. If someone touches you on the tip of a finger you know exactly which finger was touched, even if your eyes are closed; so that is a precise and distinct perception. The same thing is true for our dreams.

There is always a duality between the angelic soul and the domineering self, which is animal. If it's the animal force, the domineering self, that dominates in someone, then their dreams will be mainly animal ones. (Some people say that such dreams are purely psychic in nature.) But if the angelic side predominates, that person's dreams will have a spiritual meaning. And if the two sides are relatively balanced the dreams will be mixed: sometimes more spiritual, sometimes more animal. For example, some people don't believe in the existence of the angelic soul; they think that all our dreams are only psychic reactions in the state of sleep. Now that is false, because if we didn't have the angelic soul we would only dream like animals. Moreover, even with individuals who are uninterested in such things or who don't believe in spirituality there are still cases of dreams with a spiritual meaning, since they also have an angelic soul. But the dominant aspect in their dreaming is psychic or animal. If there is a spiritual aspect in their dreams often that needs to be interpreted by a spiritual Master; however certain spiritual dreams are so clear and self-evident they don't need to be interpreted.

The problem of dreams is like spirituality in general.

People have asked us why we haven't written about the techniques of spirituality: it's so vast that there are no techniques. There's no 'technique' for interpreting dreams: each person dreams in their own way, and each of us has his or her own personal symbols.

Dreams are one way in which the other world communicates with the people of this world. The people of this world have their habits, their symbols and ways of understanding, and those in the other world also have their symbols. For example, if Ali wants to communicate something to a Christian he will speak to that person through the symbols of Christianity. If a dream happens to be purely psychic, a psychiatrist who knows that individual well may be able to interpret it. But if someone's dreams are spiritual only a true Master can interpret them. (However, if that person is interested in the spiritual path they will also be helped to understand the meaning of their own dreams to a certain extent.)

Is it possible to distinguish dreams about episodes in our past lives from dreams that arise from the unconscious?

This question is pointless, because our unconscious contains the memories of the angelic soul ever since its creation, including all its previous lives. The soul itself doesn't forget them. During our dreams, because of the partial disappearance of the veil between the *nafs* and the soul, some of those memories can be revealed to our conscious awareness.

Can a person ask God for special favours?

That depends on your spiritual stage.

1. In the stage of exotericism, having ordinary material and spiritual wishes helps the believer to keep in constant communication with God. That is why it has even been recommended to ask God for things at that stage.

2. In the stage of *tarîqat* (the Path), the spiritual traveller takes a vow to put into practice the lesson of submission to God and His satisfaction. That's why it's better for the disciple not to ask for anything and to surrender to the

divine Will. During this stage spiritual travellers begin to realize that God knows what is best for them. For example, to set a particular spiritual goal for yourself is a mistake, since that can stop the soul from advancing.

3. The disciple knows what they can ask for and what they shouldn't request. This is the rank of *ma'rifat* (inner knowledge and spiritual understanding).

4. They have reached the end, and their will is merged with the divine Will. This is the final stage of *Haqîqat* (the Truth, the true Reality). In all of these stages we ought to ask for what satisfies and pleases God, in addition to what He Himself has ordered human beings to ask of Him.[2]

Is it harmful for a person to seek the awakening of their spiritual senses, concentration on God, love of God, and so forth? Aren't these qualities bestowed by God Himself?

When you don't know what to ask for, it's better not to ask for anything. We should carry out the divine precepts because we consider them to be our duty. That's all . . . In each soul there's a special sense which can begin to function only by God's command, which doesn't depend on any personal effort. It is called the 'sixth sense' – but in this case that term means something quite different from the way it's ordinarily used. That sense may be granted to anyone (whatever their spiritual state), and it may not be awakened even in a person with great faith. This sixth sense may be completely or partially operative, and it may be temporary or permanent. For example, there are people who have no faith at all, but who see things that will happen in the future. The sixth sense can't be increased or diminished by any efforts or practices undertaken by the individual concerned. In contrast, the awakening of the spiritual senses in each individual depends on that person's personal efforts and degree of faith, spiritual practice and above all their inner purification. The more the spiritual senses are awakened the more our Love of God increases.

How can we distinguish between the products of our imagination and true intuition?

First of all, a spiritual intuition is an idea that comes to us from outside ourselves. Secondly, it is fixed and definite. Thirdly, it has a profound and lasting effect on us. Fourth, we can't change or affect a spiritual intuition by our own will. And finally, the memory of it continues to last for a very long time.

The products of our imagination, on the other hand, come from within us, can be changed by our will, don't affect us deeply, and don't remain in our memory for very long.

THE SIXTH SENSE AND THE SPIRITUAL SENSES

The sixth sense is a special power whose centre is situated entirely in the angelic soul. Once that centre has been awakened it is independent and autonomous: it can use and control the bodily senses as it likes, or it can do without them entirely. While the bodily senses never go beyond certain limits, the sixth sense is able to penetrate things which are even beyond time and space. With the help of the 'vision' of the sixth sense, for example, a person can see through walls, view things at great distances or look within an individual and know how that person really is. This phenomenon is quite different from telepathy, because here the person who is observed doesn't even suspect the existence of what that other person sees in their innermost being.

The awakening of the sixth sense causes the person who experiences it to come to know God. This sense exists in a latent form in every human being, but it only becomes manifest as a result of God's will, and there's nothing anyone can do to bring about that awakening. This awakening can be partial or total, and it can be temporary or permanent. When it is total and permanent all the spiritual problems and questions concerning this world are answered. The person who has this gift can use it as they wish, but they will never use it for purely personal ends or to do harm.

This sixth sense includes three types of inspiration, according to the type of waves it receives:

1. The inspiration comes directly from God. In that case it is always accompanied by a tremendous bodily and mental upheaval.

2. The inspiration comes from a very lofty and exalted soul, such as those that have manifested the totality of the divine Essence. The value of the message received is the same as in the first case, but the physical shock or vibration preceding and accompanying the revelation is not so severe. This inspiration is indicated above all by a sort of tremor in the mind, a mental 'spark' that precedes the appearance of the agent who transmits the inspiration.

3. The inspiration is not accompanied by any disturabance of the mind or the body. In that case its source is not located outside the person who has it.

The sixth sense is different from ordinary clairvoyance: most often clairvoyance is uncontrolled and involuntary, the clairvoyant doesn't understand the full meaning of what they perceive, and their perception has no intrinsic relation to faith, since a clairvoyant may even be a complete unbeliever.

The sixth sense is also quite different from the spiritual senses. They are likewise an aspect of the angelic soul, but unlike the sixth sense – which only becomes manifest through the divine Will – the development of the spiritual senses also depends on each individual's own efforts, in addition to God's wishes. The awakening of the spiritual senses is a natural consequence of each individual's efforts to reach perfection. That is why the state where they are awakened is superior to the state of awakening of the sixth sense, which only happens through divine Grace.

Finally, the sixth sense is also different from what we could call the 'ultra-spiritual' senses, those which are directly related to the divine Essence. That is something even beyond the angelic soul, which concerns those extremely exalted spiritual personalities who have within themselves, as it were, an especially large quantity of the divine Essence.

The other day you spoke of humility as a sign of spiritual progress.

Humility is the awareness of your own insignificance. It's a feeling each person should develop within themselves. For example, we should say to ourselves: 'Can I really resist the events that happen to me? No. So then what am I? Nothing. I'm just another creature like the others, and there is a Directing Force Who directs us.' We should be humble in our hearts, but our outward behaviour has to be appropriate to our personality and social position. We should defend our personality, which is a divine trust, according to the circumstances of our time and place. But at the moment when we are doing so we must also say: 'O my God, I don't consider myself to be superior to this person; I am only doing this to defend my rights.' That is how a director should behave with someone subordinate, a professor with his or her students, the mistress of a house with her servant, and so forth. This is what has been called 'pride within the limits of defending one's personality'.

In order truly and sincerely not to consider ourselves superior to others we must tell ourselves that every being, by the very fact of its creation, has this potential to reach its perfection. If in this life I have something good that someone else doesn't have, I must say to myself that if that person had the same conditions that I do in life they would also be like me. For example, if I'm a scientist, writer or accomplished artist, I should know that God considers us first of all as His creatures; in other words, He looks at all His creatures on the same plane. And He also considers us according to our degree of spiritual purification, our faith, our constancy in fulfilling our duties toward Him, and so forth – not for our external knowledge or material arts and accomplishments.

As soon as we begin to realize that we really are nothing, that's the beginning of truly knowing our self. Modesty, self-effacement, humility: that is our state before the Beloved. With regard to the other creatures, and especially our fellow human beings, we shouldn't have any pride in our heart, although pride to the extent of defending our personality is permissible.

When we imagine God we can't help feeling anything but humble and insignificant. But it's much harder to be humble with an ordinary person.

In cases like that tell yourself that God considers the spiritual traveller by looking at their inner purity, their condition as a creature, and so on. Then you'll say to yourself that we are both God's creatures: if that person were put in the same conditions as myself they would be just like me, so what difference is there really between the two of us?

At first that is only a reasoned, mental state . . .

Yes, but once that feeling has become instinctive, like your second nature, you no longer have to rely on that reasoning. You naturally feel quite humble before God, and you lose that feeling of pride in relation to other people.

In the beginning you have to use such arguments, to force yourself to see this, to imagine it (because that is your lesson), until you reach the state where it has really penetrated you and become like a sort of second nature. Then you naturally lose that state where you used to compare yourself with others, because there no longer are any 'others'. The problem of those others has disappeared, and you are what's left.

But then does that mean others don't matter? Isn't that sheer egoism?

It's not a question of whether others matter or not. This

problem of comparing yourself with others comes from
your own mind.

*So there's an artificial, reasoned humility and another sort of
humility rooted in the heart?*
No, there is one humility, first at the stage of self-suggestion (mental reasoning) and then where that humility has
become our second nature. As for us, we are still at the stage
of the humility that involves a mental effort.

*Is that why we can be humble before God, but full of pride with
regard to our neighbour?*
Precisely, because mentally you say to yourself: 'God is
immense, and I am so small . . .'; but when you are around
other people, all at once you start thinking: 'I'm a musician,
a philosopher, or whatever, while that person's nothing.'
This shows you're still spiritually immature: you're at the
same level as everyone else, still not looking upward; you
haven't expanded your outlook, your spiritual vision. As
soon as you really begin to get near to God humility
becomes instinctive, and at that point the problem of others
clears up all by itself; you're no longer jealous, you lose your
egoism.

*I have the impression that certain saints went to extremes in that
regard, that they considered themselves lower than an ant, for
example . . .*
But that's just it, you really do come to feel that you're
nothing. You have to reach the stage where you feel that
you really are nothing. What are you? Who are you?
Nothing. Are you able by your own will alone to do so
much as change the colour of your skin? Those saints spoke
truly, they were experiencing the truth.

No, of course I can't do that; but neither can an ant nor a dog.

Good, an ant or a dog can't do that either. So logically we can conclude that we aren't really superior to the ant or the dog. And as for them, what are they? Nothing. So we're all nothing. You are nothing, they are nothing; so there's no reason that you should consider yourself to be superior to them.

But after all there is a hierarchy in creation: between a human being and a rock . . . ?

All the creatures have the potential of reaching perfection. But that doesn't concern us. We haven't created anything. Can we transform ourselves into a rock? No. As long as you aren't able to really create something you are nothing. Truly you are nothing. I am nothing, you are nothing. For example, some atheists say: 'But we human beings also create things.' But what do they create? Nothing at all: they transform things. Fire also transforms things.

So there is only one path of humility: the path that leads back to our true relation with God.

There's no other way. Everything starts with the effort of suggestion. Moreover you only obtain that humility through spiritual growth. When you advance spiritually and reach the stage of spiritual maturity you experience the awareness of reality, of what is truly Real. You genuinely feel that you're nothing, that you're not superior to anyone else. And at the same time you sense that you're nothing, you are very happy to exist and very satisfied with the state where you are. You are far more contented with the state where you are than when you were full of pride and thought you were something special.

Because then you've found your place?

Because at that moment you are in what is Real.

THE NECESSITY OF PERSONAL EXPERIENCE

It isn't enough just to start out on the way of salvation; you also have to find the correct path. Because if someone puts into practice a false precept, even if they do so with all their faith, they will never achieve a positive spiritual result. On the other hand a true precept, once it has been correctly applied, always reveals the esoteric truth contained within it. We have to understand that religion is essentially a science based on *experience*, including both a theoretical and a practical aspect, whose aim is our salvation. It encompasses all the other sciences, because whoever knows their self knows everything. But it is only through practising the authentic commandments or formulas of religion, one by one, that we can come to grasp its full significance. In fact the precepts of religion can be compared to the formulas of chemistry, physics or any other experimental science, though without their sources of error. If a single one of the elements is incorrect, or if you make a mistake in applying the formula, the outcome will be spiritually muddled, vague or non-existent.

That is why the writings and interpretations of those who claim to grasp religious and spiritual teachings simply with the aid of their intellect or on the basis of a purely academic knowledge arrive at conclusions that are false, misleading and sometimes disastrous. Because their conclusions are based on abstract theories and unverified personal interpretations, the truth is mixed up with errors, so that you can't be sure about anything. In all those sorts of writings and teachings you find fragments of the truth submerged in an erroneous context; only authentic experts in spiritual matters can clearly distinguish between the two.

Spiritual truths can be compared to precious gems. The theoretician is in the situation of a layman who has never learned to recognize a real precious stone, or who has never even seen one. If you mix up a few real diamonds with a handful of imitation ones, only a qualified jeweller will be able to eliminate the fake stones by examining them or testing them one by one.

All of the truths written down in this book were revealed by an experienced and perfect Master; we have only transmitted what he said. He never asserted anything without first having personally experienced it. Needless to say, some people who have not yet completely awakened their spiritual senses, or whose sixth sense has not been awakened by God, may well take the divine words to be simply personal points of view or philosophic theories. But in reality they are authentic spiritual truths discovered as the result of conclusive spiritual experiences.

For example, you can experience and test for yourself the harmful effects of pork and of alcohol, which are forbidden by certain religions. The transgression of a divine command has a very specific effect on the soul, which you can perceive if you have some preliminary knowledge of your self and a certain basic degree of spiritual awareness. Once you have made a vow to God to abstain from those foods you must pay close attention to yourself for several weeks and then break that vow (without letting yourself be influenced by any feeling of guilt that might distort the outcome). The more sensitive you are, the more you will feel the effects of the divine precepts.

It is only then, through personal experience, that you will understand why God forbids or commands certain things for humankind. Then you'll see that religion was brought for the education of the angelic soul and in order to guide the self toward Perfection. Each authentic religious precept necessarily has material repercussions as well: for example, eating pork eventually has psychic and physical effects that are proportional to the quantity consumed and to the individual's own sensitivity. Its psychic effects consist in the person's being impregnated with the lowly and repugnant qualities of pigs, such as cruelty, insensitivity, indifference to adultery, greed, brutality, and the like. Charity and love of our fellow creatures have their source in the divine light, but the heart that has been filled with these qualities becomes opaque and resistant to that light. And as for the physical effects of pork, it can give rise to various illnesses that are secondary aspects relative to its spiritual and psychic effects. The same thing is true of alcohol and other drugs. Hallucinogenic drugs and hashish (cannabis), in particular, irreversibly destroy the nerve cells of the brain, and they can make a person socially and spiritually unable to accomplish anything important at all. Their effect is to destroy those elements constituting the connection between the angelic soul and the physical organism, disrupting the co-ordination between the soul and the body.

The other conclusion we can draw from this experiment is that religious truths can only be understood and realized through practical experiences. And finally, we can see that the spiritual effects of disobeying the divine precepts are not proportional to the 'quantity' involved, but instead depend above all on the individual's intention.

When alcohol and pork are not prohibited by the particular religious law that an individual follows they only have an influence on that person's body and psyche. On the other hand, when a person's religion forbids them, then both the angelic soul and body are affected, and the quantity does not really matter for the soul: a tiny quantity can have the same harmful influence as a very large quantity. In spiritual matters it is the intention that counts, while the quantity only matters for the body. Muhammad said that 'the intention is more important than the action'; and for Jesus Christ, to contemplate adultery in one's mind was the same as actually committing it, although there are also different degrees of aggravation or mitigation concerning intentions.

There are two different ways of practically experiencing spirituality: either you can do it under the guidance of a Master; or you can do it all alone, by yourself, without a Master. That second Path is filled with dangers; it's full of highs and lows, terrible risks of defeat and failure. The person trying that route can make dozens of round trips without really advancing at all. Those who wish to explore the esoteric dimension of religion in that way should be warned: it's better to stay put and not to move at all rather than to wander out on to those icy slopes haunted by spiritual wolves and thieves.

The person who follows a true Master is always protected against those dangers, while the other voyager must fight them alone. But although it's very dangerous, the possibility of travelling alone does exist. Occasionally, although only very rarely, a soul does manage to reach its goal all by itself. Such a soul must be extremely strong and have an extraordinary capacity, and in that case the spiritual experience it has acquired will have a remarkable value.

Whichever method the seeker chooses, they must have faith, must possess exact and authentic spiritual precepts, and must follow carefully and precisely all the rules pertaining to each form of practice. They must know how to interpret the results they obtain and how to draw the proper conclusions from their own spiritual experiences and those of others as well. Therefore practical spiritual experience demands determination, a firm will, decisiveness, perseverance, a logical mind and clear thinking . . .

All of these qualities are guided by the spiritual attraction motivating that person, an attraction which is manifested in human beings either by a desire for the truth or by Love of God, or by both of those together.

The farther a person advances along the path, the clearer and more obvious their results will be. Each trial they pass increases their faith and gives rise to greater Love for God; that Love encourages them to undertake new efforts, while those trials purify them and gradually awaken the spiritual senses. That is the beginning of true knowledge of the self. Then the disciple becomes a different person, with wider perspectives and a rational logic that is able to grasp the realm of spiritual realities.

IV

THE PATH

What do you imagine God to be like?

That's something that can't be encompassed by our imagination, that each being senses according to its state of closeness to God or remoteness from Him . . . I don't know how to express it, it's a special sensation, an awareness. God is something that is everywhere at the same time. The conception we have of Him depends on the different stages of spirituality we've passed through: at each stage we have a new perception and awareness, a new experience of God. You can't say just what that sensation is, you can never define it. Sometimes you sense God, and you feel that you are also God, that the carpet is God, the wall is God, that God is everywhere. That is an absolutely extraordinary sensation: at the same time you feel that everything is God, you also know and are aware that you aren't God. Once we've become aware that everything around us is God, then we can really understand the saying 'God is everywhere'. And when we move on to another stage we have other particular perceptions: they aren't something you've simply imagined, but real, true forms of spiritual awareness that go to the heart of your soul and mind and that stay with you.

How can a person manage to reach God?

Of course for someone who is fortunate enough to find a true Master, that path seems easy. But if you aren't so fortunate it's better to avoid following people you don't really know, because that is so dangerous. If you happen to follow a charlatan or a deluded master you risk breaking your neck, spiritually speaking. So I urge you not to follow anyone you aren't absolutely sure to be an authentic Master or guide. Purify your heart in devotion to the One God and follow the teachings of an authentic religion: that is a safer way. Your spiritual progress may be slow, but it is also less dangerous. And you will continue your work in the other world, because there are also spiritual schools there and more work to be accomplished. At least you won't have fallen back while in this world. For if you take the wrong path you'll go backwards, but if you simply believe in God and listen to the voice of your heart, then you'll advance.

As for myself, I don't pretend to judge any movement or individual. God is everywhere, and there are people of God everywhere, authentic Masters and guides. In general it's true that they usually remain unrecognized or are known only by a handful of people. But besides those true Masters there are innumerable false masters and charlatans; so you have to be very careful. In this path, when you don't know who you're dealing with it's better to stay away from them: to live simply according to your own beliefs, or to stick to the exoteric side of your religion. If a person is Catholic, for example, they should go to church and follow the outward laws of their religion. If someone wants to reach the esoteric dimension but doesn't yet know an authentic Master, then it's better for them to avoid getting involved with the wrong character. That route is dangerous; if you aren't really sure that your guide can lead you safely past those dangerous pitfalls, then reason tells you to stop and wait.

By nature every human being, except for those who have already acquired a certain spiritual maturity in their past lives, seeks to dominate and control others. As soon as most people become interested in spirituality they unconsciously look for a master who can be their 'puppet'. This sort of 'master-puppet' is someone who adapts himself to his disciples' desires and whose disciples only obey him to the extent that his orders happen to agree with their own desires. That kind of master does whatever pleases his students, and they in turn are looking for a master who will do what pleases them. Their relation to him is one of pseudo-submission. Unfortunately, most schools are actually like that.

So if an authentic Master, following a divine command, does take on the responsibility of guiding others, those sort of disciples won't come to him because he doesn't want to act according to their desires: a true Master wants to put into practice what God desires. And most people don't like that because it doesn't please their domineering self. That's why it has been said that 'the master of unbelievers is the devil', because the devil really is the master of the domineering self. Such masters are actually following the path of their own domineering self without being aware of it. They claim that their path is divine, while in reality it's just the opposite.

Everyone can be controlled by negative forces, except for those with true faith. Right now the negative force is dominating this world; it isn't any particular person, but a general influence, a wider ensemble. The force of darkness and the light are always in balance. Sometimes one of them dominates and sometimes it is the other. Here on earth it is usually the negative forces that dominate. But right now their domination is too strong. We live in such an age that . . . unless God comes to our rescue. The Master used to say that those spiritual voyagers who manage to safeguard their faith, their 'Connection' with God, during this period of time will earn a special spiritual honour in comparison with all the other souls.

What is that Connection?
When God created humankind He made an agreement with the archangels. In order for human beings to reach perfection, to become totally absorbed in the ocean of divine Grace, they need to pass through earthly stages to gain knowledge and understanding. The archangels interceded for humankind at that point, arguing that given the

immense power of the negative forces and the domineering self, people wouldn't be able to complete that journey without God's help.

Therefore God made this covenant: He would establish forever a *Connection* with the people on earth. In every age that Connection is maintained by a human being of extremely high spiritual rank who is given that mission by God, who manifests God's power and reflects the divine Essence. That individual is the spiritual intermediary, the link between God and the people of his or her time, with the primary role of guiding those people toward their perfection. That person's hand is in God's hand, and only by taking their hand and holding on tightly will the spiritual voyager be safe from the attacks of those negative forces, from failing and going astray. Holding firmly to that Connection, through the most recent links in one's own time, is an assurance of spiritual success; but breaking that Connection is catastrophic.

Since the very beginning those divine persons have followed one another like the links in an unbroken chain. In addition, the current link in that Connection can designate certain individuals to guide others; but those guides are not themselves that link, since they are joined through that person rather than directly to God.

Is that Connection the best way to avoid the danger posed by 'distracting spirits'?

To have a true Master, not to break the 'Connection', and to want God only for His sake, not for our own desires: everything is summed up in that. For example, suppose that a distracting spirit comes to you and suggests something pleasing that involves one of your weak spots. It will say: 'I'm going to tell you what that person is thinking.' You'll answer: 'That doesn't interest me; it's of no use at all.' Then it will say: 'I'm going to give you power over this or that person.' You'll simply reply: 'That doesn't interest me.' Or it will say: 'We're going to show you some fantastic sights.'

Each time you'll answer it and ask: 'Do you come on God's behalf? Or on behalf of what god?' You've studied, you've learned the spiritual principles: if what that spirit suggests is opposed to those precepts you reject it. But the best thing is not to try to have contact with them at all. Someone who wants to reach the goal of the path shouldn't be looking for other souls or spirits. There's no point in it.

For example, are things like spiritual power, clairvoyance, or inner peace spiritual temptations?
Yes. It's permissible to wish for calm and peace, but we shouldn't turn such things into our spiritual goal. If an inner calm comes to us that's fine and we thank God for having granted it. The desire for spiritual power comes from pride. And except in the case of those persons who are sent by God, the sort of clairvoyance that most people ask for leads to unhappiness.

What is a spiritual addiction? For example, what about those dervishes who listen to zikr[1] and fall into a state of ecstasy?
Pleasures and ecstasies that one strives for do bring about a state of addiction. That is not our goal. Our goal is the aim of each student of the path of perfection: to rejoin God. The usefulness of zikr is as a sort of relaxation, a moment of rest for the soul in order to restore its full energy, or to make a request, an intimate prayer.

And yet the dervishes of Hajji Ni'mat[2] were well acquainted with such states.
Their attention wasn't focused on the path of perfection; they were following the lesson of obedience, and they were preoccupied above all by power and spiritual distractions. They were fascinated by the spiritual powers of Hajji Ni'matullah, and that is why after his death all of them, except for a handful who reached the goal, became disoriented and had to come back.

If someone, for example, sees or hears a guide in a dream, should they obey that person?

No, that depends. For example, if a person who has a Master sees another soul who speaks to them and gives them certain orders, they should reply: 'I'm a disciple of So-and-so. Is what you say true, and do you have my Master's permission?' In principle souls don't have the right to lie, but they can speak in a veiled or symbolic fashion, and sometimes without taking into account the particular time or period of the person they're addressing. In any case, if such souls come from the groups of distracting spirits, what they have to say always contains something that tends to please our domineering self. So if you can recognize their snares that's fine; but if not, they can lead you into the abyss. That's when you really feel the need for a true Master.

. . . For the time being most people can't assimilate everything we have to say. What they ought to know first of all is that they must believe in the One God and His prophets, and then that they should have faith in their prophet and follow and practise his principles and the moral laws which come from a divine Source. That's all they can accomplish without running the danger of falling into dangerous spiritual pitfalls. Without the presence of a true Master they can't really know anything more. It would be best if they went out and looked for a spiritual Master, one who is truly a Master; but if they really aren't able to recognize an authentic Master, then it's better simply to follow and practise the principles we've just mentioned and to try to have a personal communication with God and their prophet.

There are a great many religious opinions and self-proclaimed 'spiritual' sects. What should someone do in order to be certain that what they're following or reading or believing is really the truth?

When such a person reads a spiritual book they should first be sure their intentions are pure and then make the following prayer: 'My God, I am reading this book in order that You might guide me toward a way or a true Master who will lead me to You, because I only want what You want.' The Master says: 'We should purify our heart of every preconceived idea, whether positive or negative, and of any sort of zealotry or fanaticism, and our intention should be to approach God and surrender our self to Him so that He can guide us.' It's not through intellectual knowledge that a person is able to understand such things, but through the light of our heart, through the heart's own detector. But in order to have the right sensitivity to divine things we have to purify our intentions. The person who proceeds in this way will be left with a certain impression when they've finished reading ... And if the book in question happens to be false its contents won't affect them, or will even leave an unpleasant feeling.

There are special centres for meditation, with exercises to increase one's inner knowledge, mental tranquility and concentration.

Those are artificial methods that reach and make use of the powers concealed within each human being. Such methods do have their results, but those results are often temporary and can lead people astray. It's like a rose that you force to bloom by blowing hot air on it, rather than allowing it to blossom according to the usual process of nature. That's the difference. And ordinarily those artificial techniques also bring about a kind of spiritual addiction.

Such results are harmful for the soul, even though they are rapidly attained and immediately visible. Although those methods may create a temporary pleasure or sense of calm, they end up making the soul lazy and sick.

You used the expression 'mental tranquility', which indicates that the spiritual goal of such methods is not sound. However if such practices are prescribed by a psychiatrist, then they don't concern the realm of spirituality and can be considered as a sort of medicine or tranquillizer, in which case that won't be harmful for the soul. But if they are given by a deluded, false master, with a spiritual goal, then that will be harmful for the soul.

And what about the religious centres in India?

As for people who have not yet had an initial grounding in the authentic spiritual life, who lack a real spiritual education and the necessary degree of genuine experience, it's better for them to avoid such centres. But once they've had some experience of the authentic spiritual life, if they are interested in doing, shall we say, some spiritual research, then that's all right. But otherwise, for those who lack that background, it's better for them to stay away. I don't mean to say there aren't authentic spiritual schools in India, but simply that those who lack the necessary experience can't distinguish which ones are genuine . . . For each authentic school there are a great many others that lead people astray; so since the chances of the uninformed person happening on the right one are so slim, it's better simply to stay away.

What do you think of yogis?

There are those yogis whose aim is to acquire certain psycho-spiritual powers in order to show them off and impress others; even if such yogis live as hermits, their intentions are always tainted by a corrupting touch of psycho-spiritual pleasure. And probably there are others who are advancing along the right path. But in principle those individuals have withdrawn from the world, so they aren't publicly visible. However the Master said that if they don't discover the Connection they won't reach the ultimate goal, because the stage of the Truth (*haqîqat*) is unique and requires the Connection, whatever a person's starting point may be.

The best example is that provided by the prophets and true saints. You never see a prophet or a saint putting on a 'show', performing a spectacle in order to please their *nafs*.

WHAT SHOULD WE DO?

There are several factors that help determine each individual's spiritual aptitude: their primordial created essence, the efforts they've made for the path of perfection during their previous lives, their overall present condition, the particular age and spiritual *milieu* in which they live, and so forth. That is the reason why people's spiritual aptitudes aren't all the same.

1. Someone who hasn't yet acquired the necessary aptitude to know how to look for an authentic esoteric spiritual school runs the danger of falling prey to spiritual wolves, such as false masters. The damage that false masters can do to the souls of their disciples is sometimes so great as to be irreversible, at least in this life. It is better for such a person to stick to the authentic teachings of the exoteric dimension of their religion; and if they have no exoteric religion they should at least follow the path of their own conscience, while keeping their faith in God and the eternity of the soul.

In order to choose an authentic Master an individual first has to correct his or her own inner intentions and way of thinking and then try to see objectively just what the goal is that they're looking for in spirituality. If someone wants to obtain spiritual pleasures as quickly as possible, such as getting in touch with distracting spirits, 'seeing God' by means of particular mental or bodily techniques (meditations, dances, postures), reading other people's thoughts, having a sense of spiritual domination over others, learning about certain events in the past or the future, or just showing off their spiritual accomplishments in order to be admired; or if they want to flee their responsibilities by living as a parasite or withdrawing to some quiet retreat: in short, if a person has any of those thoughts at all it's better for them not to get involved with spirituality in any form. For since their intentions are misguided they run a very considerable risk of following deviant paths or falling prey to false masters.

2. The person who has acquired a certain spiritual maturity[3] and knows how to look for an authentic esoteric school will not be fooled by the countless false masters on the lookout for their prey. The teachings they offer won't satisfy such an individual and they'll never be satisfied until they encounter an authentic school. If they happen to fall into one of the traps of a false master, that situation will only be temporary; they'll come to recognize their error and then they'll leave. Even if such a person can't figure out just how the false master has been deceiving them, they'll sense their mistake. But once they've managed to find a true spiritual Master – whether one who is living on earth or in the state of 'soul', without a human form – then that person must establish the Connection, obey their Master and put into practice the Master's orders and precepts, which are always in agreement with the actual spiritual teaching of the prophets.

At that point there are two possibilities: either the disciple succeeds in correctly applying those precepts and in passing all their spiritual trials, in which case they will reach a level high enough to be saved from the cycle of successive earthly lives; or they don't completely succeed in following that teaching. In the latter case they mustn't despair and give up, and above all the disciple must not break the Connection with his or her Master. God only asks of us what we are able to do, and advancing even one step toward Him is better than doing nothing. In an authentic spiritual school there is always the possibility of what is called a 'leap of the soul'. This act of God's Grace, which disciples often benefit from after a difficult trial, consists in the soul's suddenly being moved ahead by one or more stages. For example, a person who felt unable to fight against their *nafs* will suddenly feel stronger and more capable.

By correctly applying the divine teachings and continually fighting against the domineering self the disciple will gradually become able to control it. Once a person has reached that point the veil separating the angelic soul from the body will gradually begin to disappear. The spiritual senses are awakened, and that person comes to know their self. It is through knowing the self that they will be able to know God. And it is from that point on that they will truly come to know the *Valî*.[4]

The stage leading up to knowledge of the self is often extremely long, and if someone claims to be able to see God simply by means of a particular technique or form of meditation they are mistaken or fooling themselves. Until a person has reached the stage of really knowing the self they don't have the ability to tell whether what they're contemplating is actually God or not (although there are certain exceptions . . .).

This power that is called the awakening of the spiritual senses only reaches maturity gradually and through a natural process. The inner calm and more or less constant ecstasy caused by such artificial methods are harmful because they tranquillize the soul and keep it from advancing towards true knowledge of the self and true knowledge of God. There is no state of rest in the process of spiritual advancement, and the soul is always subject to the contrasts between high and low, hot and cold. When the first signs of knowledge of the self appear we become aware of who we are, where we came from, what we are supposed to do here, and where we are headed. Then the disciple has the possibility of knowing the different stages: mineral, vegetal, animal, and the stage of the self. And they can also know their preceding lives, see the invisible world and the spiritual hierarchies (to the extent of their soul's rank), and a great many other things as well. Sometimes a Master, for reasons known only to him, doesn't allow certain things to be unveiled to the conscious awareness of his disciple; but the disciple still keeps securely within himself all the kinds of knowledge and capacities that belong to that particular spiritual level, only in a potential form.

Is it necessary or advisable to know about Islamic culture or Islamic mysticism in order to understand your teachings?

These teachings are divine principles, the same principles that have been mentioned by all the prophets. The religions only differ in their secondary aspects; focusing exclusively on those aspects won't lead you anywhere. The stage of the Truth is unique, is only One. Islamic mysticism is the most recent and richest form, but you won't get anywhere by relying solely on the secondary aspects of religion.

Can someone follow these teachings even if they don't have a specific religion?
A person can follow the path that has been outlined in the book *The Path of Perfection* without accepting one of the so-called 'religions' created by men which are widespread nowadays. But the person who finds that book pleasing and who would like to follow that way already has religion, because the true religion is to love God and to want to be near Him. To try to follow His commandments transmitted by the prophets *is* the true Religion. By 'commandments' I mean those which are truly His commandments, not the ones that have been made up or transformed by men. At present it is the religions created by men that predominate here on earth.

Do you accept disciples from all religions and all races?
I myself am not a Master, such that I could accept disciples; I am a student who only repeats what he has actually practised and understood from the teachings of his Master, because that is my duty. All of the authentic religions come from God. The value and dignity of human beings have to do with the purity of their soul, not with the colour of their skin, the form of their body, their social position or wealth, and things like that.

What do you think of someone who believes in this path but who doesn't want to be connected with it officially (for example, because of the behaviour of certain disciples)?
When I speak to you about something 'official' I mean official in a spiritual sense. I've already told you I'm not a

Master, but a disciple with the task of maintaining the Connection. The person who draws close to a true Master, in addition to the spiritual advantages they gain, can also benefit from the Force that flows from his physical presence. That Force penetrates the disciple's spirit, as it were, and strengthens it ... If it isn't possible for the disciple to be physically near their Master, then the Master will arrange things, with God's help, so that the disciple can benefit in other ways. That only happens, though, if the person truly wishes to be near their Master but doesn't have that possibility. Thus what really matters for the disciple is maintaining the Connection and actually practising one's faith.

The answer to the other part of your question is as follows: in order to judge a school first of all you have to study quite closely its master, not the individual or collective behaviour of certain disciples. By definition, a student goes to a spiritual school in order to come to know and correct his or her faults and weak spots. On the other hand, individually observing each student is useful in many other ways, which would take a long time to explain in detail. For example:

1. Seeing their strengths and weaknesses helps you to know yourself better.
2. Knowing them more intimately helps you to discover whether a school is true or false.
3. It helps you to know the hidden aspects of the Master's personality, to uncover his negative points if he is a false master, or to reveal his positive points if he is an authentic Master, and so forth.

How can a person start out on the path without immediately accepting the Master, and without having had more convincing experiences?

As long as you don't know the truth about a person, you can't and shouldn't totally entrust yourself to them. Moreover, in order to know the Master completely you would have to have a very high spiritual rank, so you can only come to know the Master gradually.

Within each person there is an inner voice that guides us. If someone truly wishes to gain God's satisfaction, with all their soul, then they will gradually come to trust their Master, assuming he or she is an authentic Master. But if there is some defect in the disciple's intention and they're really looking to satisfy their own *nafs*, then they're likely to run across a misleading, false master. How can you recognize the characteristics of a true or false master? By referring to what has been said about that problem in the book.[5] Of course to want God solely for His sake is impossible at the very beginning; but with the help of our will and through actual practice we must gradually come to purify our intention.

As for those personal experiences you mentioned, they must also be grounded in authentic spiritual teachings.

Is it possible to work with a representative of the school, but without relying on the Master and the school itself?

The Master is always spiritually watching over his school. The Master says: 'The Truth doesn't have any need for propaganda. He who watches over the school takes care of it and guides whoever deserves to be guided.' The guides he has designated maintain the Connection, and the students can work with them. The responsibility of the servants of the school is to organize the gatherings and to transmit his messages; but from the spiritual point of view they are like the other disciples. There is only one difference for the servants: if they have the authorization of the person responsible for the school they can also guide others, within the limits of their particular mission.

If someone feels they have a mission to help others toward the Truth, can that be something suggested by the distracting spirits?

A person can only guide others by God's command. A disciple can only guide if they have received permission from the Master or the person responsible for the school, although that person can answer questions about the teachings they've received, within the limits of what they've personally experienced.

Can students of the school guide other students who are less advanced?
If they've received permission to do so, yes.

What is the situation of those who come to understand a spiritual school later than others?
Seniority alone isn't any sort of criterion; you also have to take into account what each person has previously acquired, the particular efforts they've made, and the role of the divine Regard. Some students can make enormous progress in a short period of time. And there are other longtime disciples who can turn into 'esoteric bigots'.

What is an 'esoteric bigot'?
The Truth is one, but it appears under different veils according to each person's degree of purification and spiritual perfection. The process of perfection is an uninterrupted, continuous movement, stage by stage. That is why the teaching within an authentic spiritual school develops quite rapidly. Although the basic principles don't change, each day brings new lessons, so that if you ask the same question after a certain period of time you will receive different explanations.

Now at every stage of spirituality, in the exoteric side of religion as well as in the esoteric dimensions, you'll notice people who have come to a halt and become stuck in the stage they've reached. Since they're unaware of their condition they think that they possess the Truth, that they're on the right path and are even making progress. Their mind has a certain limited capacity, and as soon as it's filled they can't accept anything more. So they become self-satisfied and unteachable; nothing new can affect them any more, and they reject out of hand whatever doesn't agree with their old ideas. Those ideas themselves are mistaken, because if they had truly assimilated and realized their spiritual teaching they would have understood the true principles that would have allowed them to go on to the following stages and discover new aspects of the Truth. Their ideas are like an outdated calendar that has become useless for finding out where we are in the current year.

The examples of bigots and 'esoteric bigots' are quite numerous throughout history, especially in countries where religious traditions are well established. For example, it was in the name of their religion that the Pharisees refused to recognize Christ; and similarly, Christians and Jews would not have neglected the Qur'an if they had penetrated the deeper meaning of the Bible.

How does someone become an 'esoteric bigot'?

The source of that state is pride. In the presence of a powerful spiritual Master such a disciple is unable to manifest their pride outwardly. Such a person should try to purify themselves and to transform that pride from a blind and unconscious state into a condition of spiritual dignity and awareness of their personality. But certain disciples don't work at that task, so that their pride, instead of being purified, is simply repressed deep down inside them. Eventually it comes back out in the form of an obstacle that blocks their advancement and stops them at a certain stage. That can happen during the Master's lifetime, but usually esoteric bigots only reveal themselves after their Master has disappeared, with regard to a successor they find it impossible to accept.

Some esoteric bigots are passive, inactive and only do harm to themselves; but others are active, try to spread their ideas and become dangerous for other disciples as well. They are spiritually ill, and only a powerful shock can cure them: sometimes they react to that, and sometimes not.

You've mentioned several groups of spiritual students. What is the basis of those categories?

There are the genuine students, those who thirst after the Truth and who truly make a great effort to follow all the precepts. They are the real disciples; they accomplish a great deal of progress. There is another category of students who do intend to follow all the teachings of the spiritual school but who aren't able to; they are like people who want to stop smoking, but who can't manage to quit. However they can continue to follow the school because they do have faith in their Master and the authenticity of his teachings: that is what is essential. They should continue to follow the path, while waiting for those spiritual leaps that will enable them to work like the students in the first group.

There are still others who believe in the school, but not in the same way as the first two groups: they have a sort of parallel faith. They are convinced that the teaching is true; they agree with the school, even though they don't follow it. They haven't yet obtained the necessary degree of spiritual maturity. Then there is the group of those who aren't aware of the school. But if they do read or hear about these spiritual teachings they approve of them. We must believe they have within themselves the capacity to follow the divine path in their own religion. And finally, if someone denies what is said in this school that person doesn't yet have the inner capacity to advance actively toward perfection.

There are also various other groups, such as the ineducable ones, the fickle-minded, and so on.

I have the impression that when someone is in the school they also benefit from the divine favour with respect to their material problems.

Yes, but that doesn't concern us, precisely because you don't want the school because of material advantages. You are concerned with the essential goal, which is Perfection. In any case, even if someone senses that, they are still obliged to struggle. And in addition, the school is not involved with the material affairs of its students. Perhaps those 'advantages' are simply the result of the discipline that the students apply in their everyday lives, which attracts the divine Grace.

You've said that there are people who come here, for example, to solve their problems of personality.

That is their initial motivation. But once you've understood a spiritual school's lessons, what they imply, then you can gradually change your outlook, your point of view. The Master said that certain people became martyrs in order to gain paradise, and then they were shown that there is something even better than paradise. At that point some of them were satisfied with paradise, while others, once they had seen the two possibilities, preferred to come back and continue the path of perfection.

That's how this school is. The person who enters it will see that there is Truth there. Then the choice is up to them: if they really desire the Truth they'll continue the path, and that's fine. Or if that doesn't really interest them, if they can't or won't put it into practice, then gradually they'll give it up.

Can the same lessons be of benefit to both young and old, educated and illiterate, city people and peasants?

You won't find any two individuals who actually receive the same lesson. But you can tell them, for example, the general rules, and each person will grasp what they're able to assimilate. At the outset it is a general teaching for everyone. But eventually, as the disciple advances along the path of self-knowledge, each student's lessons become more and more different from the lessons of others.

What is your basis for judging a disciple? That person's desire to love God, their spiritual capacities, their knowledge about the path?

A true Master looks at the disciple's heart. He sees each person's hidden side and judges them accordingly, and his judgement is infallible. He sees their angelic soul. Actually I wouldn't dare use the word 'judgement'; rather we should say the Master's 'expertise' (or some other synonym), because only God is able to judge, or someone to whom God has specially entrusted that power.

Could we say that the way of thinking of Europeans is guided by reason, and that of Easterners by sentiment and feeling?

Every potentiality exists within us. The state of each individual depends on the particular potentialities they've cultivated. If someone follows their feelings, then intuition is stronger; and if they follow reason too much then they have less intuition.

When an individual is enslaved by their reason they only accept things that can be clearly grasped by the physical senses. But in order to understand spiritual problems we have to use the spiritual senses that are latent within us. Now the more the physical senses predominate in us, the less the spiritual senses become manifest. While the physical senses are already awakened by nature, we have to make a special effort to arouse our spiritual senses. It's because many Westerners are used to judging according to the logic of their five physical senses that they are sometimes more receptive to spectacular demonstrations and pseudo-spiritual techniques from various sources than they are to authentic spirituality.

It is essential to develop the rational aspect of spirituality, but first of all you need to have a certain inner, intuitive divine Love which should guide us. You have to study and gradually put into practice and experience for yourself the precepts of divine science taught by an authentic Master. Then after a while you will start to develop the spiritual senses of the angelic soul, so that thanks to them you will be able to begin to reason in a 'two-dimensional' way. In my opinion it is very difficult to get those dominated by their reason started off on the path; but once they have 'taken off' they follow the road more securely. As for intuitive people, they start off more easily, but they also run into more dangers than the others.

Westerners don't like to bow down before another person and show their admiration the way disciples of Eastern masters do.

Those Eastern masters who consider themselves superior to others, who encourage their disciples to bow down before them and who perform public demonstrations of their powers, aren't true masters. A true Master, despite his immense spiritual power, is very humble. That sort of public spectacle is demeaning to his dignity.

Every angelic soul loves to show its respect to souls that are superior to it. Our present-day society has artificially perverted this natural human inclination so that instead of adoring the saints, who are superior souls, people bow down before social idols and myths created by other men. The mentality of those who have been conditioned by the mass media is educated to believe and trust nothing else; so they worship and bow down before the idols manufactured by the media, instead of being concerned with genuine values. That's why so many false and misleading 'masters', by using the methods of publicity, are able to make themselves worshipped by great numbers of people who then neglect the true saints. Westerners do know how to worship the demigods of the media; the way they prostrate themselves may look different outwardly, but the reality is the same.

God knows how much I detest flattery and false modesty, but when I sense God's presence somewhere, I bow down before Him.

Europeans, and Westerners in general, seem to be scornful of Easterners.

Perhaps that is because those Easterners have neglected their strong point, which is spirituality; they have been blindly infatuated with Western technology, and they haven't realized that this sort of ideology which neglects people's spiritual dimension leads to a dead end. The West, in order to free its people from that dead end, will also have to be more concerned with human beings' spiritual needs and look to the East for help.

Authentic spirituality creates a strong personality, and there is nothing to prevent a person from studying and applying modern science and technology while safeguarding their spiritual personality. The two sides are really complementary. Spiritual science is the goal of every human being. Material science is a means to ensure the well-being of the human body. People need both of them. So no group should be scornful of others and proclaim its superiority. We are all human beings, and each people should use its special abilities for the well-being of all.

The Eastern ambience is favourable to the work required by spirituality, while the Western environment encourages a more concrete, material aptitude. Thus each group can make beneficial discoveries in a spirit of mutual collaboration, without any feeling of superiority or inferiority.

Everything has its normal course, and the best path is the natural course. The person who wants to take a shortcut will end up going over the cliff. The normal way in spirituality is to live as the prophets lived: to live among other people and to be useful to them, to take care of your body as well as the soul. No prophet went around teaching spiritual techniques. So this is the normal way: to have a life in society like everyone else, and to carry on the inner work for yourself. Outwardly you are like everyone else, but inwardly you are different. And in any case, how do those people who use techniques of meditation and concentration know that they've found God? They haven't followed the normal course of their growth. It's as though you were to take your small child for a walk somewhere: both of you see the same things, but you're the only one who really understands. You know what that place is, while your child is unaware of it although he has the same senses you do. So he'll believe whatever you tell him.

Techniques of meditation have the same sort of effect.

They lead you to a place where you don't belong, like a child who hasn't yet acquired the necessary development and understanding required by that particular place. You happen to see something and you think that it's God. But you don't really know whether it isn't the devil. What is the difference between God, the devil and spirits who are just making fun of you? You don't really know. But someone who develops naturally will acquire the power of spiritual discernment they need to distinguish God from the devil.

In order to come to know God you have to fulfil the duties He has established for every human being, and you have to wait for yourself to develop normally. You have to be patient. All children have the desire to be like grown-ups, but they don't grow up any the faster because of it. If you make your child grow artificially you'll only make their body bigger, not their mind and spirit. They'll just become an unusually big child. Those who perform ascetic practices in order to communicate more quickly with the spiritual world are like such big children. They may communicate, but they don't know with whom or what. They pretend to be happy, to have this or that special power and so on, but those are the words of children. They want to impress others with their powers, just like children.

Some of them are more capable than others, but those abilities must also be developed in a normal, gradual way. If you see people who have become enlightened all at once, that is because they have already done their work. They completed their spiritual growth earlier and have come back to this earth for certain special missions. They come back, and then at the appropriate moment, like a lamp, they are connected to the spiritual current. Now you can connect just about anything to an electric current, but that won't necessarily give you light. The natural development of the soul can take place during a single lifetime or in a hundred lives or more, depending on the particular individual's aptitude and personal efforts, social *milieu*, and so forth; but it is gradual. There are certain exceptions: sometimes God wants a being to be enlightened in two hours or in ten days, but we can't generalize from such special cases.

Is there any assurance that a person who has made a real spiritual effort will rediscover the right conditions that are required for continuing the path during their following life?

If someone has reached a certain level in their spiritual work they are kept on in the other world in order to continue their work there. That is a special favour: their spiritual development will take place in the other world. But if someone hasn't reached a sufficient level to stay there they'll come back. Some people have that assurance and others don't.

But in that case, below a certain level there's no reason to bother working!

To begin with, who really knows their own level? Moreover you can't say that it's not worth working, because every effort has some kind of result. And in any case, you have to pass this stage you're in; you aren't able to *not* work. Finally, the individual who has worked will have a better spiritual *milieu* in their following life than someone who has not worked. They may become the child of a religious person, for example, and yet still fall into materialism: once they've come back to earth there's no guarantee. However for those who have made a pact with an authentic Master, it's their Master who will take care of guiding them.

If someone comes from an unfavourable *milieu* and still reaches spirituality, that is because of the good quality of their earlier work. The person who has worked in that way will come into contact with an authentic spiritual school during their following life, but it will still be up to them to take advantage of their opportunity.

If someone withdraws to the mountains, away from other people, is it easier for them to fight their nafs?

No, from our point of view withdrawing from the world

and living as a hermit is not an effective way to fight against the *nafs*.

What should we do in order to avoid pride and becoming stalled on the path?

When a sensation is mingled with pride, that comes from our *nafs*. You can have the most extraordinary sensations and still be quite humble. When you realize that your power doesn't come from yourself, but from another source, how can you have any pride? But if you think: 'God gave me this power because I deserved it . . .', that 'I deserve it' comes from pride. Because if we look at ourselves objectively we recognize that we can't even accomplish our duty.

Everything we do in this school belongs to the realm of duty. We can't do anything more than our duty. If we try to do more that rebounds against us: it's like making a motor run faster than its normal limits. The person who advances beyond their capacity goes very quickly for a little while and then comes to a halt, without mentioning the other pitfalls that are possible.

Many other spiritual paths claim to go beyond accomplishing one's duties.

They're not doing their duty; they're doing something else: they're entertaining themselves, seeking special powers, pleasure, looking for ways of enjoying themselves. They've set themselves a particular goal. As soon as you set yourself a goal it's all over, you're stopped. The soul wasn't created so that we could set a specific goal for it, because God hasn't limited its ascension, its progress. But as soon as you set a goal for the soul you've limited its advancement.

What is the spiritual method called 'chaplarî'?[6]

Chaplarî complements the method of *râstlarî*. *Râstlarî* is the method in which all the statements and predictions made by a specific spiritual source turn out to be exactly as we had imagined and understood them. *Chaplarî* is the opposite:

although the statements and predictions announced by a trustworthy spiritual source are true, they don't take place in the way we had understood and imagined. An authentic, perfect Master uses the method of *râstlarî* to win over and reassure his student's heart; after that, by using the method of *chaplarî*, he vaccinates the disciples' souls and strengthens their faith in order to prepare them to reach the stage of submission and abandonment to God and to follow unquestioningly their agreements with God. The souls of disciples who are only used to *râstlarî* are like unvaccinated children, and their faith is vulnerable. But once they've been tested by the method of *chaplarî* their faith becomes firm and invulnerable, which is to say that they've been vaccinated against the various temptations and diabolical tricks of the domineering self and its allies.

To summarize, we could say that *chaplarî* is a sort of vaccination of one's faith against the negative force. *Râstlarî* is indispensable for those who are just beginning in spirituality, in order to form the core of their faith and to prepare them for starting out on the path of perfection. But once they've become students of the path of perfection, unless they've been vaccinated against the negative force by the method of *chaplarî* they will become ill and grind to a halt after the slightest attack by the negative forces. Only a perfect Master is able to utilize both these methods. However we must stress that an authentic Master never uses real *chaplarî*, but rather establishes a sort of pseudo-*chaplarî* in order to vaccinate his disciples. A true Master never lies.

But in any misguided path the disciples involved with a false master who is mistaken are always ready to invoke 'chaplarî' in his defence.

The perfect Master should first use indisputable forms of *râstlarî* to reveal his true spiritual personality, so that his disciple will be certain that he is a true Master. The lesson of *chaplarî* can only come after that. If you study your Master's personality closely you can distinguish perfectly well between a true and a false one. A false master is an insulating barrier between his disciple and God. There is an undertone of pleasure for the *nafs* in everything the false master does or says or predicts. With a true spiritual Master, on the other hand, it's just the opposite: he transmits the divine current to his disciples' hearts in an amplified form. Every order he gives tends to hold back the domineering self and control it, and he's like a bridge that the student can cross to reach his goal. But false masters, on the contrary, try to create a bond of dependency between the master and student by using different psycho-spiritual techniques appealing to the powers of the *nafs* in their disciples.

In addition, you can tell when a master has a worldly interest in what he's doing.

How can we know when we're faced with a case of chaplarî?

Once our heart has become sure that our master has full spiritual powers and is not a liar, then if he makes a prediction or gives some information that doesn't turn out the way we expected, that is *chaplarî*.

Can a promise from the Master be chaplarî?

The Master's promises inevitably come true. He can promise you something but not indicate the time frame, so that the promise is not realized in the period of time you had imagined. What he predicted for you will happen, but not in the way you had originally understood it.

The Master doesn't want his disciple to come to a halt. If you are stopped by a promise, he will use *chaplarî*. A student of his school shouldn't stop; we must keep on advancing. As soon as a disciple is sure about something, there is a danger that very assurance will stop them. So spiritual students must avoid becoming attached to anything. They mustn't halt along the Path. There's no pleasure for the *nafs* in *chaplarî*; it's a vaccination against the enjoyments of the *nafs*.

Shouldn't we stop to work on our weak spots?

What does a weak spot have to do with *chaplarî?* You ought to fight against your weak spots, but you shouldn't turn them into an obsession . . . We have to become used to fulfilling our duties without asking for anything more.

When we are faced with certain problems we don't know how to act or respond.

First of all you should correct your intention and look to see if there haven't been any similar cases in the Master's teaching. If there really haven't been any, then make sure your intention is pure and go ahead and act. If you are mistaken you haven't lost anything, since you have gained another experience.

Should we wait for signs?

There are always signs, but sometimes we don't understand them. You have to be on the lookout for signs.

Can a person ask for a sign?

Yes, it's good to ask for a sign. If God wishes He will guide you, and if He doesn't want to, then He won't. But you shouldn't say: 'God, I absolutely must have a sign!'

Isn't spiritual rank related to proximity to God?

Yes, but we mustn't turn that into a goal. A person who is on the path of perfection must have all their attention focused on the path. For the beginner the game of spiritual rank is useful as a motivating force; it can create a state of spiritual self-respect in them that gives them the energy needed to fight their domineering self. It's like with children, when you give them a certain strength of personality that helps them to advance; but when you've gone farther in spirituality your humility begins to grow and the desire for power becomes weaker.

Is there a special method to recognize the Valî of one's time?

No. Either your spiritual senses must be awakened or else it is through the divine Will.

Isn't it easier for those who have known the Master personally to form some conception of his spiritual personality.

No. The person who truly seeks will find him just as well as the other person. And if the Master wants to make himself known he will do so. There are a lot of people who saw him and didn't really know him, and there are many others who never saw him and yet who know him.

A Muslim invokes the Prophet and the Imams in his prayers.

We do that too. There are also people who worship other saints. You can see God in everything, even in a human being. At that precise moment this object, or this person, manifests the effect of God; that may only last a few seconds. If you have the right eye for seeing God you can worship Him in whatever you see. Do you see God in your Master? No, you don't see Him there, that's just your self-suggestion. If you really do see Him, worship Him . . . But if you don't, no: obey Him. Just as Moses saw God in the burning bush: if you see Him, fall to your knees and worship God wherever you see Him. You have to forget the particular persons and only remember Him. Otherwise you will become trapped in complications and never be able to find your way out.

If you want to perceive God – through your Master, for example – then don't limit God. You have to see the divine Essence, the Infinite, through this form which you know. Perhaps someone else has glimpsed Him in another form . . . As long as you haven't reached the stage of the Infinite you have to concentrate on what you can see that reflects the Infinite. Think of the body of the Master as a sort of window through which you can see the Infinite, or else that becomes idolatry and polytheism. There is God, and then there are the teachers, shepherds, spiritual Masters: God is

Unique, and all the others are means to Him. Don't go looking for endless gods – there's only One.

Can we concentrate on you in our prayers?
No, not on me or on anyone else; that is false. I am only a student like you.

INNER PEACE

Inner peace has always been the goal of human beings. In order to reach it people have used various means that we can divide into two main groups: material means and spiritual ones.

Material means influence the person's psychic dimension; they are transient and unstable, such as wealth, power, social relations, occupations, the various forms of security created by different societies, and so on.

Spiritual means influence the soul itself. They can be divided into the following two main categories:

1. The psycho-spiritual methods, such as meditation, spiritual dances, or the life of withdrawal from the world are particular techniques. They have a calming effect on the psyche that lasts for a longer or shorter time, but they are dangerous.

2. The genuinely spiritual means: this is the path of the prophets and saints. These methods make the soul healthy, and they also have an influence on the psyche. Among these spiritual means the method of *râstlarî* creates perfect inner peace, but it can also stop the spiritual voyagers on their path.

The best method is that of using *râstlarî* and *chaplarî* together: along with the basic background of inner peace the disciple feels, there are also the jolts and upsets created from time to time by periods of *chaplarî* that keep the spiritual traveller from taking their *râstlarî* for granted.

Our Master's method consists in keeping the student from

going to sleep, spiritually speaking; it educates them so that they understand their full responsibilities and don't stop with a particular discovery, spiritual state or way of acting. At the same time that the disciples have a state of inner peace, they never become locked into a single method or way of acting; at each instant they discover through actual experience the appropriate ways and means that they must select according to the particular new situations in which they find themselves, which are tests they undergo in order to advance in the path.

In this method, as soon as a student wants to remain satisfied with his or her temporary inner peace the Master reawakens them with jolts that pull them out of that state of calm for a while, because permanent and absolute peace can only be attained once the soul has reached perfection.

V

SPIRITUAL PRACTICE

The aim of each person who comes into this path should be to fulfil those duties God assigned to Adam and his descendants in their original covenant, so that they can reach perfection. Those duties are as follows: we should accomplish everything that is good and everything the Prophets have commanded on God's behalf; and we should avoid everything that is evil and everything the Prophets have forbidden. The religions differ only in their secondary aspects, but they all follow the same central path and have the same goal. The spiritual traveller should follow the thread of God's manifestations among human beings until they reach Him; they need to seek the help of an authentic, experienced spiritual Master to guide them toward their perfection. The duty of this school is to guide human beings toward perfection.

Our own duties can be summed up in the following three categories:

1. Spirituality: the rights of God, or our duties toward Him, such as the acts of devotion and everything else that brings a person closer to God.
2. Society: the rights of our fellow human beings. The spiritual traveller must respect the laws and other rules and should be his or her own policeman.
3. Morality: disciples should follow the rules of morality and keep their conscience alert; that creates respect in others and also has its reward with God.

The student of the path should follow and carry out all three of these kinds of duties, and if they fall short even with respect to part of those duties they will be held responsible for the consequences.

What are our duties toward others?
Our duties toward others are already included in what I've just said. Follow *God's* commandments: that is the answer to everything.

Do we need to ask in order to find out what we ought to do?
With regard to our duties, we need to ask God for His approval and guidance, and we have to want to satisfy Him. But as for wanting anything else, you should refer to the precepts of religion and the path. In any case, since we try to fulfil our duties toward God, He will ensure that we have everything we really need.

We ask because we're not sure whether our duty might perhaps consist in doing this or that particular thing . . .
If you've been taught that it's your duty to ask, then do so; but first of all learn what to ask and how to ask. God says: 'Pray to Me so that I may answer you'.[1] However, that formula is subject to certain conditions, and they can only be fulfilled if we have carried out our duty as His servants.

Can we ask for help to do our duty as a disciple?
That's not something to ask for, but rather to put into practice.

We can ask for His help?
As soon as you fulfil the duties you consider to be God's commands you automatically attract His approval and His help. Ask His approval for everything you do, and the moment will come when you will realize with certainty that nothing at all is done without His approval.

*But if we no longer have anything to ask Him for, we no longer
have any relation with God!*

What do you mean? You have a relation with God all the
time, since you are carrying out your duties. When you do
your duty you are always in the process of thinking why
you are doing this, why you aren't doing that, of telling
yourself: 'Because God wants me to do this, because He
wants me not to do that . . .' That's the relation with God.

In order to fight the domineering self you must continually ask God for His aid; and when the *nafs* has broken
loose, plead for your Master's help. However, that last
guideline only concerns those disciples who are completely
devoted and attached to their Master.

It is preferable for a student of the path not to ask God for
material things, because God already knows what we need.
If we deserve something, if it is in our best interest, He will
give it to us. I've had the experience of that myself: when He
gives something because we've asked for it, it would be
better for us if He hadn't given it. It isn't a very pleasant
experience: you have what you wanted, but you're in a state
where you wish you hadn't received it. So it's better not to
ask, and even if you do ask, to trust in what God wants.

You didn't ask for material things?

Yes, precisely that. Of course that is a personal experience, and perhaps there are others who haven't shared it. If
it helps you to strengthen your communication with God,
then do ask Him. And of course there are many other things
which He Himself has permitted us to request, such as the
forgiveness of our sins, the desire to satisfy Him, His help in
struggling against the domineering self, to plead for salvation, that He not put us to the test, and so on.

*But when you sum up the path as 'doing your duty', it seems so
simple that one wonders why people have said so much about
spiritual paths – or is it so complicated to carry that out in reality?*

Precisely, just what are those duties? That's the whole

problem. It's like somebody asking: what is medicine? You answer: recognizing illnesses and treating them. That's easy to say . . .

But couldn't someone have written down a complete list of all our duties, once and for all?
There is the stage of formal knowledge (*savoir*) and the stage of true understanding (*connaître*). The divine teachings and principles have been written down everywhere. After you've separated the true from the false you can learn them all by heart, and then you will 'know' them; but in order to really understand their effects you have to experience them for yourself, to put them into practice. That's when you begin to reach the stage of true understanding. True understanding means really knowing those principles in all their details. Those are personal impressions, particular experiences, which are very difficult to communicate.

Truly understanding our duties involves both a theoretical and a practical, experiential side. It's like learning music or any other art. You really have to work, gradually and progressively, in order to learn the truth about each thing. Because we don't have words that are exact enough; there aren't any words that can faithfully communicate those ideas. So we have to listen to these words and then put them into practice so we can truly understand their real meaning. That's why, even if you write these words down, how can you know whether you've really understood their meaning until you've actually put them into practice for yourself. There's no other way for you to know. You learned music. How did you learn to play? By reading a book?

No, I chose an instrument and just started to play.
All alone?

All alone at first, and badly; after that I worked with a teacher.
So the teacher taught you the meaning of this and that. Could you communicate to non-musicians what you've

learned since then simply by writing a book? No, you can only transmit that knowledge to someone who has already learned music.

That's why the person who has travelled through the different spiritual stages understands what the Qur'an means, not someone who has never had anything to do with spiritual practice. Such people want to interpret the Qur'an as soon as they've learned a little Arabic or some Arabic grammar, but even a professor of Arabic literature couldn't really comprehend the Qur'an. The Qur'an can only be truly understood by someone who has first learned the spiritual 'notes' or 'alphabet'. Because the spiritual alphabets are quite different from our ordinary alphabet. Somebody told our nine-year-old son: 'You should be afraid of God.' He replied: 'We shouldn't be afraid of God, we should feel ashamed before Him.' He's right: we should be ashamed of ourselves. And what we've just said about the Qur'an also applies to the messages of the other prophets.

What I transmitted in the book (*The Path of Perfection*) is for beginners. When you've advanced a little along the path your ideas also evolve.

For example, in whatever I do I have the impression that I don't even manage to fulfil my duty. So of course I would necessarily be quite ashamed to ask for something else in exchange, like a sort of business transaction. But that realization only comes gradually and you have to work at it. When someone is only beginning, they need to think about reaching perfection. If they expect to receive something from God in exchange for whatever they do that's all right. But once they've reached a certain level their ideas will naturally change and evolve, simply through their becoming conscious of their self and aware of the larger situation.

If a person is able to work on that by using mental suggestion it can help them to reach this point even more quickly. For example, you begin to tell yourself that in whatever we do we don't even manage to fulfil our duties. Right now you still expect something in exchange, because you believe you're accomplishing many other things in addition to your duty. There's no harm in that, but all the same try to get rid of the idea that you're managing to accomplish even more than your duty. For beginners that is something extremely difficult. You shouldn't try to force them; on the contrary beginners need to be encouraged in the other direction. What I've just described only applies to those students who've already passed through the first stage and entered the following one.

Why do we have a duty, in relation to what?

Out of nothingness God has given us existence, and He has set out the path for us to follow in order to reach the supreme Goal. So that we can reach that goal, He has assigned us certain duties which were accepted by Adam and his descendants. God has given us a free will, the power of discernment and the ability to distinguish between good and evil. He has entrusted us with His Breath, His Spirit, and breathed It into us; and thus He has given us a superiority over the other creatures. What difference is there between us and the animals? Are we the ones who created the animals and plants? No. Then can we use them to our own advantage gratuitously, without any justification?

Since God gave us a certain superiority over them, we also accepted certain responsibilities. Of course somebody could always object: 'I don't want that advantage.' But do you really want to return to the stage of a rock that everybody walks on? If you do then that's fine; you would no longer have any duty. But in that case what could you accomplish, what could you do? Nothing. Think about that; look at things clearly.

Perfection means reaching the truth of things as they really are. Those conventional, agreed-upon 'truths' that people have created for themselves aren't really truths at all; we have to discover the real truths, the genuine truths. You have to tear open the shell of this conventional personality that society and your surroundings fabricate for you, which

keeps you from actually seeing what is real. That condition-
ing is what prevents us from seeing reality as it truly is. For
example, some people don't see any difference between a
dog and a person as far as their inner value is concerned; the
dog is an animal, and so is the person. But we say that the
human being, because they bear the divine Breath within
them, is superior to the animals. However, for someone
who hasn't had this religious education the dog and the
human being are equals.

*How can a person win additional points or special honours in
the path?*

In order to acquire honours, if you are sent to school, it's
your duty to study. If you study very well you will win
certain awards. In the path of perfection it's the same.

In principle it's impossible for us simply to get to the
point of accomplishing all our duties. However God creates
certain opportunities thanks to which we can win extra
merits or honours. Take advantage of those occasions. If you
diligently fulfil your duties you will have opportunities to
win additional points. But you shouldn't expect any reward.

*But these duties we're supposed to fulfil, aren't they simply
those of the exoteric side of religion?*

God has given us a body thanks to which the soul can
reach perfection; therefore it is our duty to take care of our
bodily hygiene, to exercise, to eat what is healthy. And we
must also avoid things that are toxic or harmful for our
health. For example, if you don't drink alcohol you won't
suffer the damages resulting from alcoholism; and in addition, if that is also forbidden by your religion you will have
obeyed a religious commandment at the same time as you
have fulfilled a duty towards your body. So when you fulfil
a divine duty you gain both a material advantage and a
spiritual one. Just like an employee who goes to work: they
also fulfil their duty.

But they receive a salary for that!

In a way, you also receive a salary. Your salary is that your soul is in the process of growing and developing. You accomplish your duties, so you will have a normal growth; you will get closer to perfection. Those who fulfil their duties better will grow more rapidly, which is a great advantage.

But in that case shouldn't we do a great deal more than the minimum of things we accomplish in this school? I'm thinking of people like the ascetics, Sufis and the like.

We are neither a particular sect of Sufis nor a group of ascetics. We are spiritual travellers in the school of perfection. We can't even fully accomplish all the duties of this school, not even our normal duties, so how would you hope to do something more? More of what? There isn't any room to do more. Who can do more than that?

Those who spend all their time in meditation or in prayer, for example.

That is a great mistake. Certain Sufis try to reach the goal by means of asceticism and inner visions. The ascetic chooses to withdraw from the world, to mortify his body and to pray. The pious person seeks his salvation in the ritual prayers. The Sufi, the hermit, the ascetic, the pious person – each of them is seeking to reach the Goal in their own way. But in order to get there you also need the Connection. God brought us down from heaven and placed us in this earthly body so that we could acquire the substance needed to reach perfection; without that body the angelic soul can't grow and develop towards perfection. The soul and the body are like two feet that the self uses to advance. According to the teachings of religion we must live in society, create a family, be useful to others, and so forth. So to withdraw from those individual responsibilities in any way at all – whether it is the life of a hermit, a certain type of Sufism, constant meditation, or anything of that sort – is to lose one of those feet; it means going against the original covenant between God and humankind. We mustn't neglect the rights of the body in order to gain spiritual enjoyments.

I don't mean to say that there haven't been Sufis, hermits, ascetics and others who've succeeded in making contact with the Connection. Perhaps in the past those methods, although they are very long and dangerous, were once permissible. But the circumstances of time and place have evolved since then, and those methods are no longer adequate or adapted to the people of our own age.

And yet those individuals do such extraordinary things, they see the other world . . .

But how does that help them to advance? In this world a small child sees and hears the same things you do, but does that child understand the same things? What's important is to understand what you feel, what you see, what you hear. Otherwise, as for simply seeing things . . . The essential thing is that the person understands what their senses perceive. Let's suppose that by performing certain exercises you've succeeded in contacting the world of souls. If you haven't also acquired the requisite spiritual development you'll understand nothing of what you see and hear, except for the harm that may do you. The souls of dead people are people who have lived like us, and they've kept the same ways of thinking, except that now they've become invisible. But I ask you: what more are you going to get from seeing the dead than you already know from your contact with the living?

If you're looking for the path of salvation, the prophets and saints have clearly shown it to us. But if you're looking for spiritual powers and enjoyments, or seeking to satisfy your pride and vanity by showing off your superiority to others, then woe unto you! When you eventually go to the other world, in addition to all the other sins you've committed, you will have to account for one of the greatest and unforgivable ones: voluntarily depriving your body of all the permissible blessings that God had provided for it. Because depriving yourself of eating, sleeping, or forming a couple are difficult and painful things to do; and if you've undertaken such things on your own, without a religious commandment or an order from God, you will have a very heavy responsibility to bear.

Now since the spiritual accounts of the body and the soul are separate, the soul will have to respond to the complaints of the body. But what will such souls reply? Suppose that you've beaten a dog for no reason at all; the dog will bring its complaint against you. How would you answer?

You could say that the human being is superior to the dog, so the dog has no right to complain.

But in what respect are human beings superior? They're superior only if they obey the rules of their superiority. Otherwise they're actually inferior to the dog. You consider a teacher to be respectable as long as they know their subject and do their duty; but if they neglect their responsibilities they shouldn't expect to be respected. So a person is superior if they behave like a truly human being, like a saint (because their superiority is related to the purity of their soul). But if instead they follow their animality, which is far more savage than a dog's, are they still superior? In order for an individual to be acknowledged as a truly human being they must follow three basic foundations: the religious laws, the social laws and the moral laws (their conscience).

The human animal (*bashar*) is the highest animal on earth, so how can we respond to the body's complaints in the other world?

We come into this world with a debt. The person who doesn't pay their debts won't deserve mercy. When someone gives you a benefit or an advantage you become indebted to that person. One person may become director of a company, and another becomes their employee. The director has different duties to the employee, but each of them has to fulfil their duties or they will be replaced by someone else. Our situation here is similar. People have become the 'directors' of the earth, but if they don't accomplish their duties toward God, Who gave them that advantage, then they'll lose it.

Are our duties toward God different from our duties toward society?

With God we are in the relation of a servant to his master. Our duty toward society is to see what is good, say what is good, desire the good, and do what is good (that is, to respect its laws and rules).

We should transform ourselves into a sort of 'machine' for doing our duty. The person who becomes like that will continue their path safely and with certainty until they reach their perfection. We must respect our duties in every area of life, whether with regard to society, our family, religion, and all the rest. When a person reaches that state a sort of divine dignity is created within them. They become ashamed to expect anything in exchange for doing their duty. We ought to transform ourselves into that sort of person, not into the mentality of a child or a trader who does a good deed and immediately expects a reward in return. Fulfilling your duty gives you discipline, stability, nobility, patience, dignity, everything.

How can we find the boundary between our duties and our pleasures, since we can often interpret whatever we do to be our duty?

In general doing your duty, at the beginning, is not a pleasure. It's only after a person has made a certain amount of progress, after an inner transformation, that they can truly distinguish between pleasure and their duty. Before that people are often mistaken, but gradually they begin to distinguish between the two. The licit, permissible pleasures are necessary. What is harmful is to have a weakness for pleasure. As soon as you have a weakness for a particular pleasure you know that comes from the domineering self, the *nafs*. People don't have a weakness for doing their duty.

Can you do your duty with a sort of pleasure?

Why not? Satisfaction isn't forbidden; you can be satisfied to have done your duty. When fulfilling your duty becomes a second nature then you do feel a certain pleasure from it; and when you fail to accomplish your duty you feel like you're missing something.

Sometimes you feel worn out, without the slightest desire to do your duty. That's because your desires haven't been realized; what you were wishing for hasn't happened. You have to move forward slowly on the path, with persever-ance and a great deal of patience and endurance, like a camel who has to cross a vast desert without any oasis. Your desire doesn't disappear, since otherwise you wouldn't be able to continue your activity. Desire is necessary in order to make us active, but we also have to have patience.

How can you manage to undertake something if you really don't want anything, if you're completely disinterested?

You must tell yourself that you have a duty to fulfil here on earth, that you have a mission to accomplish in order to return to your permanent home. All you have to do is to 'save up' for the next world; tell yourself you have a real personal interest in fulfilling your duty.

Can you have a personal stake in doing your duty well, in wanting to do it well?

Yes, you should have a stake in accomplishing your duty in just the right way; that's enough. 'Having a stake in it' means that you're expecting a reward either from God or from people around you. But whether we're doing some-thing for God or for other people, we shouldn't expect our reward here in this world.

Isn't the satisfaction of doing one's work properly already a form of attachment?

No, it's simply being assiduous in your work, and that's good. Someone who is diligent and assiduous with regard to material matters will also be that way in spirituality. It's legitimate to be satisfied in such a case.

It is written in one of the Master's books[2] that he only once asked God for something particular, and that he regretted that for the rest of his life. Should we take his example as a model and never ask God for anything?

That depends on your spiritual stage. In the stages at the beginning you can ask for everything. But once you've worked and advanced to a certain point you gradually begin to feel that you no longer need to formulate requests. That is a higher level. In the book[3] it is written that one shouldn't ask God for particular things, but that precept is intended for someone who has reached the condition of absolute surrender to God. Until that stage, everyone has wishes. When a person is starting out on the path it is quite legitimate to ask for things. But the more the student advances, the more they'll come to know God and the more they'll realize that there's no need to ask Him, because God will give them everything they need without their even asking for it. As long as the disciple hasn't reached that level, that inner spiritual security and confidence, they can ask God for something, but their requests should be expressed in the following way: 'O my God, I ask You for this thing . . . but I surrender to Your will. Do what is right for me.' We have to become used to not protesting whenever the results aren't what we were expecting. That's a good method for getting into communication with God and a good way to start fighting the domineering self.

Are charity and self-sacrifice subject to certain conditions?

To accomplish acts of charity and self-sacrifice without any concern for the practical outcome, but simply in order that God might be satisfied with us, was also the teaching of Jesus. It is the teaching that emerges from the Gospels. There is no point in scaring people so that they won't lie or break the law; they should do what is good by nature, devote

themselves entirely to others for God's sake. But uncon-
ditional charity and self-sacrifice are a very advanced teaching applicable to those who have reached the stage of complete surrender to God. Until we reach that stage we also
have to take into account such particular conditions as the
time, place, individual capacities, and so on. That is why
self-sacrifice and charity toward everyone and under all
conditions is far from a harmonious state of equilibrium.

Be charitable, but also don't ignore your duties toward
your self, your family, those who are near to you, your
society, and so forth. You have to know what is each
person's due and learn to do each thing in its proper place.
That's a bit more difficult than simply practising charity
without any distinctions. It requires a charity that is
balanced, harmonious, exactly appropriate to the situation.
Going to extremes, without the right measure – anybody
can do that. But knowing how to do each thing appropriately, in the right place and proportions: that's what perfection is. In every case your inner intentions should be charitable; you should love each being, want what is good for
everyone. But in each particular case you also need to
understand the nature of the situation and apply your power
of self-sacrifice in just the way that is appropriate to that
situation. You have to find that proper equilibrium, or else
you won't be able to reflect and act correctly.

Each thing has its place. For example, a student of medicine may know that this sort of medicine is right for fighting
this or that disease, but the most important thing is recognizing the proper dose for each particular case. We all know
that charity is something good, but how and in just what
proportions should we apply this charity in practice? True
understanding means knowing the right proportions that
are appropriate to each thing. In the exoteric religion they
don't give those proportions, they only say that this medicine is good against that disease: but in what doses, under
what particular conditions, for which sort of patients . . . ?
But in this path we do speak of such things, and we are

obliged to learn them. When you make a mistake you are warned about it. The closer a person comes to perfection, the more extensive their field of knowledge and understanding, the more they act appropriately, in the right proportions . . .

When you've discovered that equilibrium you know it. When you've finally reached the point of knowing, you *know* that you know. Sometimes you have to experiment, to try out what works in actual experience, while in other cases you can draw the proper conclusions on the basis of earlier experiences. The struggle against the *nafs* is the basis for all our work. That struggle teaches you what are the right proportions. We have to come to really know the domineering self, to fight it and learn how to combat the negative forces without going beyond what is appropriate. The *nafs* doesn't leave us; it is with us as long as we are alive. When we die it stays here, but we still carry its consequences along with us.

Does everyone have the ability to be charitable?

That's a gift every human being possesses from their very creation, unless it is suppressed as the result of later complications. Excessive charity can make us lose our balance, and we've always said that perfection is in the right equilibrium. Nothing excessive is good. If someone has too great a charitable impulse they need to restrict it; and if they don't have enough, then they must cultivate and encourage it. Charity comes from God: He is the truly Charitable One.

We should develop the divine qualities within us: in God there is everything, and everything can also come to be in us. We need to transform ourselves into a particle of the divine in order to rejoin that Whole.

Some people say that we have to become angels.

God has assigned us a higher goal. The angelic soul is in us so that it can become perfect and rejoin God. The angels are missing one aspect: they only have purity. Take gold, for example: you can't make a useful tool out of pure gold. Iron, on the other hand, is quite hard, but it also rusts. But if you had a metal as hard as iron and as pure and incorruptible as gold, that would be a perfect metal. We have to become like that.

When you're looking for the right balance you're already struggling against the *nafs*. The angelic soul has to take the qualities it needs to become suited for perfection from the earthly *nafs*.

Is it possible to use reason against doubt?

No, you can't reason with real serious doubt. But with minor doubts, the kind that everyone experiences, you can use reason. There is a kind of doubt, for example, that comes from a high degree of culture, from a wide-ranging intellect; such people are constantly reasoning and making comparisons along the path. Someone who accepts their duties toward God even in the face of doubts has more merit than the person who is without any doubts.

Does that mean we should encourage doubts?

If it's the sort of doubt that drives you to be precise and makes you advance in the path, then yes. There are curable doubts, and there is a kind of doubt that is an incurable disease. If the doubt isn't an illness it will clear up. But when doubt becomes a disease, a weak spot, then that person is unable to follow any path; they will die with their doubt.

How can we fight such doubts?

The best thing is simply to reject them. You have to be a dictator with your domineering self, not listen to it and not reason with it. You can present it with arguments, but it will come up with other ones against you. With the domineering self, arguments aren't enough: you mustn't listen to it.

Does that mean we shouldn't reason at all?

We're always involved in reasoning. Are there any situations where we aren't reasoning? Of course there is a stage where it is spiritually useful to reason; that is the stage you reach when you are quite advanced: your spiritual senses have been awakened and you have sufficient spiritual experiences, enough facts, to give you the adequate basis for reasoning. But as long as you don't have those spiritual experiences it's preferable not to rely on reasoning.

Beyond that stage one falls into the state called divine Love. At that point everything else disappears and the following stages cannot be crossed with reason, but only through Love. Those are the final stages.

You've said that we shouldn't set ourselves a particular goal, because when we reach that goal we won't be able to go any further. But in everyday life we're forced to establish goals all the time.

Here on earth you can set a particular goal for yourself because you know the value of that goal. For example, you decide your goal is to become a teacher, a wealthy merchant, and so forth. But in the case of spirituality what do you really know, how do you know what goals you want?

What do you mean by a 'balanced' way of thinking?

Don't lock yourself into a rigid set of ideas for or against certain material affairs, or else you may have to suffer the indirect consequences of such an attitude in the long run. For example, suppose a particular social or political system displeases you. By thinking about it long enough you come to detest that system, and that hatred gradually permeates your heart; since you are a believer your wishes are transmitted to the spiritual world. God works with the people's thoughts and ideas; their thinking constitutes the basis for His work. You don't do anything; you simply hate that system, but if God someday wants to overthrow that system and replace it with another one He will use your thoughts, along with the thoughts of other people like you. That is contrary to the principle that a student of the path of perfection should entrust absolutely everything to God, without forgetting that we're responsible for what comes from us.

On the other hand it is permissible to wish for the general well-being of society, without specifying any particular means or system.

Shouldn't we concentrate on the idea of perfection?
Focus on the idea of perfection since that helps motivate you to act, but develop your patience.

What about the struggle against the nafs?
You should constantly keep in mind that you have a deadly enemy within you, the domineering self.

You've said that there are people who understand, people who don't want to understand, and others who aren't able to understand, who are ineducable. Why is that?
What prevents people from understanding is their domineering self and its allies. Which is to say that they deceive themselves: they like to do certain things, so they try to find confirmation for those things through reasoning. For example, when we talk to someone about a spiritual problem, that person interprets what we say within themselves in the way they want, not the way it really is; they prefer to follow their own desires. Such a person can be educated, but that is a very difficult process.

The ineducable person really doesn't listen at all; they're just the way they are, and nothing anyone says seems to reach their brain. They just do whatever they want. I know some people like that who haven't changed since they were born.

But in that case what reason do they have to be on the path?
I don't know; you'd have to ask God why He has put them there. They have faith, but they are ineducable.

Is it too soon for them?

No, this path is too difficult for them. They don't understand; it's in their character. This school has all the different types of people. Those who are ineducable also make up a category. Even their faith is like that: they can't be influenced, whether positively or negatively, so you can't make them lose their faith either. One has the impression that their brain has been locked tight, blocked up. God closed it and nothing can get in there; that's just the way they are.

Is it preferable not even to try to understand, rather than to run the risk of being influenced by our nafs?

You have to practise these spiritual precepts in order to understand them. If you don't put into practice what you've heard and learned, then you don't really know it.

As long as a person has faith, can they be kept from coming to the school?

No, not as long as they haven't broken their Connection. We don't exclude anyone. Our school is a purely spiritual school. He is the one Who directs it. If someone becomes unworthy of remaining in the school God will decide that for them. He Himself will take care of removing that person . . .

All the prophets and saints have recommended that we ask religious and spiritual questions. Asking questions is a sign that a person is advancing. Our activity and practical experience are what give rise to questions. Those questions increase our knowledge, that knowledge motivates movement and activity, and that movement results in progress along the path.

However I rarely hear you asking questions that arise from your own experience. You're always asking general, philosophic questions: that's a sign of immobility, of stagnation, for the spiritual traveller. Your questions indicate that what really interests you is only increasing your stock of theoretical knowledge. For example, if one of you begins to doubt, you don't look within your self for the source of that doubt and what you need to do to oppose it.

How do you think you can advance if you only listen to the answers instead of putting them into practice and trying them out in your own experience? You can't expect to reach the Truth without moving ahead.

It's just that we're never sure we've understood correctly . . .

In order to understand properly you have to experience things for yourself. You're not sure of what? As soon as you accomplish your duty that's where certainty lies; the rest is unimportant. Learn your duties and then put them into practice. What are those duties? Nobody asks me a question like 'What is my duty?' That's a sign of decline, don't you see? It's been a long time since I've heard someone ask a question indicating they'd really been working . . . When you're working spiritually there are always questions.

We're always looking for what's wrong outside of ourselves, while all the faults are there inside us. As soon as we make a mistake we want to blame someone else, even though the source of that problem is within us. For example, when something bad happens to you (an upsetting incident, a misunderstanding, an unpleasant experience, etc.), instead of trying to analyze why it happened, what your own role was, you always say: 'Well, that was God's will, it wasn't my fault.' You have to try to draw the appropriate lessons from everything that happens to you. Every week all sorts of things happen to you, you experience dramatic moments, there are meaningful incidents, accidents, other events. Try to analyse the significance of those events through yourself, taking as your starting point the principle that the source of all those faults is within us. Look for that weak spot, that particular fault.

How can we recognize that this or that fault, among all our shortcomings, was the cause of this particular event?

You only say that because you're not yet working on yourself. You have to concentrate on your self, try to get to know your weak spots, your faults, your good qualities, how you are changing. That potential exists in everybody: as soon as you really concentrate on the problem you'll discover the solution.

But practically speaking, what do we need to do? Observe ourselves, study ourselves?

Yes, every night before you go to sleep carefully think through everything you've done during that day; that's a good beginning. But again, it's clear you haven't really been working or you never would have asked that question. As soon as you start to work on yourself you'll find the right answer after a while. Whatever I say here would still be another theory for you: you listen and think it sounds good, but as long as it doesn't become grounded in your own practical experience it just goes in one ear and out the other. You only want to learn these things in order to gratify your domineering self, so you can say 'Yes, I know that, but they don't', so that you can be proud of knowing so many fantastic things. But what's the point of that? It's only to increase your conceptual knowledge, but you don't bother to put it into practice so that you can really know and understand. Look at all the people who keep asking: 'Will you give us permision to go on pilgrimage?' To perform the pilgrimage as a *kirdar* (a good action, spiritually good deed) is fine, indeed it's an excellent experience, but you have to fulfil all its conditions in order to have a positive result. And you should look for the pilgrimage that's within you as well.

What do you mean, the one 'within' us?

I could explain that for you, but it would only be another theory to add to all the others. In fact I'm sure that if someone else asked you that question you could give them a whole lecture on the subject. When you've worked on yourself you come to have a certain spiritual maturity that can't be explained in words. It's an organic whole. The person who works acquires that spiritual maturity, and those who don't work on themselves won't get it. It's a particular intuition, a kind of awareness that can't be explained. Don't keep on forever asking 'how', 'why', 'what', 'how'. Everything has been said and re-said, repeated a thousand times . . .

Whenever we succeed in aligning the wavelength of our heart with the divine transmitter, that is the pilgrimage.

You've said that we should react to everything in the same way, whether things are pleasant or disagreeable.

That isn't possible, you can't do it . . . What I said was that we should *try* to be like that, that we have to struggle within our self not to say anything. We can't yet control our sensations, our feelings, but we are able to control our tongue. When unpleasant things happen to you, you are able to not say anything. Then at a more advanced stage you can even control your sensations. To summarize, the spiritual traveller should try to have control over the reactions of their feelings in response to good news and bad.

Does that mean we should become indifferent to good things?

Not indifferent, but in control. That's also a particular inner awareness, a sensation you actually have to have experienced in order to know it; it can't be expressed in words.

How should we behave with regard to the various temptations and waves of doubt that pass through our mind!

The beginner should drive them away by force, just as you would chase an intruder out of your house and slam the door in his face. But once the spiritual traveller has acquired irrefutable proofs of the truth of their way through their own spiritual experiences, then they can try to use reasoning to repel those doubts. But in order to reason against those doubts you need absolutely solid foundations, so as soon as you feel that your reasoning is not convincing them you need to treat them just as you did before. That constant struggle against the domineering self has to continue until we fully control it.

Often it seems that we're basically convinced, but then some distracting, interfering thoughts come along.

If you're bothered by those distracting thoughts it's because you haven't really managed to convince your doubts ... In the beginning you have to behave like a dictator with your *nafs*. At a more advanced stage you can act like a philosopher and reason with it – but with exact reasoning, like $2 + 2 = 4$. For example your *nafs* may suggest to you that your Master is a charlatan. You reason as follows: a charlatan, by definition, is someone who always acts for a material goal, whose deeds don't live up to their words, and so on. Try to find compelling arguments. You have to convince your *nafs* in the same way you would convince a materialist. But until you've reached that stage you have to behave like a dictator. Look to see if there are any indications that the Master has tried to guide you, to bring you together with him, because of some material or mundane interest. When you've seriously explored spirituality and have solid proofs, then you can argue with the *nafs*. Has the Master ever asked you for some material favour, have there been any indications that his path or his teaching are misguided? Are his words and his deeds in agreement? Is his teaching the same as that of the saints and the prophets? Therefore he isn't misguided.

You need to know the teachings of the holy scriptures and the distinctive signs of each truth in order to make the appropriate diagnosis for each particular case. That is the stage of spiritual reasoning, but we haven't reached that yet. In short, you can't reason with the *nafs* using only the logic of the five physical senses. In order to argue with it you need to have reached the stage of true spiritual understanding and be in the realm of all ten senses: that is to say, you must have obtained the awakening of the spiritual senses through personal experience and actual practice of the principles of the path. Until then I don't think that you can succeed in convincing the *nafs*. Whenever there's a conflict, that's because we're still living according to the logic of the five physical senses. So we need to treat the domineering self in a dictatorial manner, doing the opposite of whatever it tells us concerning each point in question.

So we can't reach that stage as long as we haven't worked, as long as we don't personally have all the necessary elements?

Exactly, you've already understood a little. We have to be firmly grounded, to have a solid grasp of spirituality, or otherwise we can't reason with it properly.

In everyday life it is our duty to do what is good. Everything that you consider to be good is only part of your duty; even being enthusiastic is still part of your duty: we have to do things well. But there are some people who want to do too much, who want to gain supplementary points.

If we set ourselves certain tasks to accomplish, does that mean we want to do too much?

Not if you consider them within the framework of your duty: then that too is positive and beneficial. For example, when Hazrat-i Shaykh,[4] who is currently responsible for the school on behalf of the Master, entrusts you with a particular task or service, and someone else to whom she has said nothing wants to do the same thing on their own initiative without having received an order, or wants to take over someone else's task, then that's a sort of spiritual greed or covetousness. Spiritual striving and competitiveness are good, but spiritual selfishness and jealousy are very bad.

Since we usually don't know, what is the best method for fighting the nafs?

You have to counter its impulses and promptings, fulfil your duty and patiently wait your turn.

How do we know what is too much?

If you examine yourself you'll find the clue. For example, when the success of others upsets you, that's the sign that you're jealous. That's the way you can know . . .

But there are always certain individuals who are in the first row, so to speak, when it comes to receiving a spiritual task, and others who sit back and wait for that to come to them.

Those who are in the first row are there because they have a healthy, active soul; however it is also essential that their intention be solely to satisfy God. If they only do it in order to have something to pride themselves about, then they risk losing the spiritual benefit. As for those who sit back and wait, if that's because they are shy then they need to fight against that. But if it's because they lack spiritual motivation their soul is lazy or weakened; in that case they should have themselves treated by a spiritual doctor or seek out the company of more active students. Then there are also the uninitiated ones who are still unaware of the tremendous advantages to be gained by being entrusted with such tasks and services.

You've said that we aren't working, and it's true. So sometimes we imagine that maybe we should leave this school, or that even if we don't leave there is nothing more for us.

There's no point in leaving the school. Even if you don't work, the very fact of protecting yourself from external temptations is already a considerable accomplishment. However you can do a little more. You need to be more enthusiastic, more active, more willing to do your duty. If your present surroundings aren't favourable, then associate more with those students who are active and fervently involved. Carry out good deeds, do your prayers in a regular, disciplined manner, read the authentic holy scriptures. All of those things will help you neutralize the numbing spiritual influence of your *milieu*.

If we begin to examine our daily life we start to realize that there isn't really room to do anything more than carry on our life from morning to night while trying not to overstep the limits, to behave reasonably, to keep the right balance . . .

That's it. If you can concentrate on living as God wants you to, that's already the right work. Try to be charitable, good, generous toward others. Try to purify your intentions with regard to others, make an effort not to speak ill of them, not to criticize them, not to judge them. We are constantly judging others. We mustn't repeat behind someone's back things we would be ashamed to tell them to their face. Nor should we do secretly the sort of things others would consider vile and shameful.

But when you're good and charitable with others you have the impression that they're constantly taking advantage of you.

No, be good and charitable inwardly, and keep the proper balance. We have to change ourselves from within. For example, you should personally detest robbery, but it's also necessary that the thief, or whoever commits acts harmful to society, be punished according to the law so as to preserve the social order. Unrestrained charity would urge you to let the thief go; but balanced, appropriate charity orders you to hand him over to justice so that he can be educated, without being mistreated. You have to become good in the depths of your being, within your self: inwardly you pardon him, and as soon as you feel that the person has been sufficiently punished there's no longer any point in bringing the law to bear as well. The aim is to desire the good for others through a balanced, appropriate charity.

In material matters, though, you need to approach people with a certain caution until you have sufficient evidence to the contrary. Whatever happens, however, you should always keep in mind that excessive goodness and generosity for a spiritual end will never be wasted.

We're told that we should pay attention to our actions. But a person can be attentive in several ways. For example, you can remember that a particular action is reprehensible, or imagine that others are observing you, see yourself from the outside, or feel God watching you.

If you can reach the point of imagining God constantly watching over you, of seeing the ugliness of earthly life, with its temporary intoxicating pleasures, in contrast with the lasting and euphoric beauty of the other world, that will automatically drive you to seek to satisfy God in everything you do. If your modesty is exaggerated that won't do you any harm in the path, but if you go too far in the direction of pride you risk a disastrous fall. The golden rule of the spiritual traveller is to be humble toward everyone; that is an excellent protection against pride and the dangers it entails.

In order to fight against that pride people who tend to put themselves first in everything should recall their own impotence in the face of events: they should remember that there is a Ruler Who governs everything, and that they themselves are only creatures like all the rest. They should ask themselves whether they can even change the colour of their skin or keep themselves from dying. They should remind themselves that the other creatures share with them the same conditions and that they have the same potential for reaching their perfection. So in that case why should a person believe that they're superior to others?

That is part of the movement toward truly knowing our self. Truly being humble means being that way toward both the Beloved and all the other creatures.

Could you tell us, the French people in the school, what are our main faults?

For you, excessive individualism, selfishness, a lack of effort for the welfare of others, self-conceit. Those are the sorts of things you need to work on. By self-conceit I mean being disdainful, proud, indifferent to what happens to others; you never feel inferior to anyone at all. That self-conceit gives you a feeling of superiority. Try to develop some modesty instead.

Can't you recognize a person's spiritual level by certain signs, even without being able to 'see' or 'know' it?
You can't know it. That's a judgement that isn't based on visible realities, but on spiritual ones.
A disciple who has managed to reach a certain level of intimacy with their Master has the right to ask about their own spiritual level, and the Master shouldn't conceal that from them.

But if someone really is superior to another person how can they remain humble with regard to that person?
God looks at the spiritual voyager from the viewpoint of that individual's creation, their piety and devotion, and their inner purification, not with regard to their formal knowledge and material accomplishments. Someone like that should tell themselves: if God had wanted, that other person would also have had the same conditions I've enjoyed and they would have acquired the same things I have, because all human beings have the potential to be able to reach this same level of advancement. And that applies to all the other creatures as well. If that person can really become convinced of that they'll lose their illusions and come to their senses.

But what if you see someone stealing or committing bad actions?
You aren't even aware enough of what you yourself are doing to know whether you wouldn't do the same thing if you were placed in those same conditions. Perhaps you don't steal simply because you are afraid of being caught, or because you aren't forced to do so right now. You can't really tell. As long as you don't even know your own self, take the healthy position, the side of precaution, when faced with other people you don't know. Be humble; don't rush to judge and don't condemn them.

Isn't there another position between being humble and believing you're superior to others? Can't you simply not think about them?

No. Your own behaviour is necessarily the result of your judgements. You're constantly comparing yourself with other people. You do it so continuously, you're so used to it, that it's become an automatic, unconscious reaction.

But out in society everyone does that. If we put ourselves in a position of humility we'll be letting other people take advantage of us.

We're talking about inner, spiritual humility; your social behaviour should be in accordance with your particular situation, personality and social traditions. It's within yourself that you shouldn't consider yourself spiritually superior to others. Otherwise you have to behave according to your own social personality. Professionally speaking, a company director is superior to a doorman and should behave accordingly. But within himself the director shouldn't believe he is spiritually superior to the doorman. Within his own conscience, morally, psychologically and spiritually, he shouldn't feel that he is superior. He's a human being, and so is the other person. But there's no point in externalizing that awareness, because then there wouldn't be any obedience and the order of society would be disturbed.

But if you see someone who isn't interested in spirituality, at least you know they aren't very advanced, even if you don't judge them to be inferior . . . ?

But how do you know that they aren't interested in it?

Some people seem to be especially materialistic.

And yet sometimes those materialists perform actions that you wouldn't be able to do in your whole life. I mean acts of remarkable goodness and generosity, of true charity. We can't judge anyone's beginning or their end, which is why it's prudent not to consider ourselves spiritually superior to others . . . Myself, when I first left for France to continue my studies I thought I was superior to all the French as far as the social sciences were concerned. When I discussed those things with other people, after a few minutes they stopped talking and didn't reply, so I thought that I'd convinced them. After six or seven years in France I understood that they hadn't even bothered to respond to what I said, because it was so unfounded.

You're able to compare yourself to others with regard to the problems you know well, things you have learned about through your five senses. But spiritually speaking we should remain neutral and not judge at all. Suppose you come to visit me after you haven't seen me for a number of years, and that I leave you waiting at the door while I receive a beginner before you. That's where the spiritual comparisons start to come in. You tell yourself: 'Here I've worked all these years while this other person is just a beginner; why didn't he see me first?', and so on. But perhaps that other person is closer to God than you are. Work on the faults I mentioned earlier. Try to fight them: above all, be charitable toward others, less selfish and egotistical; think a little bit about other people and leave behind this state of self-conceit that is in each of you, so that God will permit you to do good to others. Individualism and selfishness only increase your jealousy; so you don't want anyone else to advance, you only want yourself to stand out . . .

And what about us, the Americans?
The Master said: 'Americans are *bîmubâlat*', that is, they are careless in their behaviour. They are very enthusiastic in spiritual things, they quickly have faith and they follow seriously. It's unfortunate that they so often fall into the hands of 'masters' who've only mastered the use of the media.
Those creatures who have free will can raise themselves

from one level of creation to another, or they can lower themselves. But in order to raise themselves they need the necessary spiritual means. In order to enter the best spiritual school or university you have to have sufficient spiritual resources; in that case God will take care of your 'tuition'.

What I've just said is only a figure of speech to help you understand a little better the right procedure we should follow. Unfortunately, the media have helped form your mental outlook and steered you in whatever direction they wanted. Even if Christ himself descended from heaven you wouldn't pay any attention unless that was covered by the media. On the other hand, just about any charlatan can gather thousands of zealous disciples in short order by using those same means. But you can't reach the Truth through such methods. You have to open the eye of the heart in order to be able to recognize what is real. It's really a terrible shame to see so many well-intentioned people become the victims of charlatans and false masters. But at the same time, whenever they do encounter authentic spirituality they are steadfast and diligent workers. That's how you can acquire enough spiritual resources to be able to choose your path, your school or your spiritual university. In order to pay our 'expenses' we have to have the necessary spiritual means, and they can only be obtained by fulfilling our duties.

So there are also wealthy people in the next world?
Of course there are wealthy ones. The absolute Wealthy One is God. The closer you come to Him the richer you are and the more power you really have.

Are spiritual riches inversely proportional to material wealth?
No. A person can be rich in both respects or poor in both respects, or rich in one way and poor in the other. The essential thing for someone who is materially wealthy is to control their fortune and not to be dominated by it.

THE STORY OF THE SEVEN COMPANIONS OF 'QAVALTAS'

Seven disciples of Sultân[5] decided to spend the three days of
their annual fast with their Master. This fast always takes
place during the winter. They started out on foot and
reached the summit of the mountain called Mount Shâhû,
which is a few miles from the village where Sultân lived.
Then they decided to stay together on that mountain peak
and have their spiritual gathering there, saying to themselves: 'Since we have come all this way to see Sultân, he
could just as well come and spend these three days here in
our company.' So they waited there, but Sultân, who had
been informed of this by an invisible voice, became angry
with them and sent them a snowstorm. The seven disciples
resisted it and remained faithful to their pact, and they all
ended up dying in the snow. After three days, while they
were still buried under the snow, Benyâmîn (one of Sultân's
closest disciples) interceded with him in their favour. Sultân
forgave them, and God brought them back to life; then they
remained close to Sultân, who established in their memory
the three supplementary days of fasting which are always
observed by the devout Ahl-i Haqq each year.

These are some of the lesons we should draw from this
story:

The crucial point is their perseverance, their resistance to
difficulties. They followed their decision to their death. You
think things over, and when you are convinced that what
you are doing is in accordance with religion you must hold
on and continue to follow it to the very end. The other
positive point is their unity: they were all united by their
pact, and they remained faithful to it. Therefore you should
first think things over; but once you've made an agreement
with yourself or with God you should honour that agreement, even at the price of your life.

When faith reaches a certain level of certainty a person
can make an agreement with God. They were absolutely
sure of their faith, or they wouldn't have dared to do

something like that. But there is also a negative lesson in that: they shouldn't have insisted on imposing their wishes on God. That is why they were killed by the snow.

When they saw that they'd made a mistake, shouldn't they have changed their mind and been less obstinate?
Perhaps they weren't spiritually mature enough. That was their weak point. They relied on their faith, but their way of thinking wasn't yet mature. The first fundamental lesson in the path of perfection is to surrender to God's will, not to try to impose our own wishes on God. That wasn't an act of resignation, of surrender to God; that shows a lack of spiritual maturity. God became angry with them, but He also forgave them and rewarded them. They shouldn't have asked that of Him, but God still gave them back their life and the maturity they needed. As for us, we say that we must fulfil our duty without asking for anything.

So a person isn't responsible for their lack of maturity?
No, of course not. And this story shows that when we rely on true faith, even if we make mistakes God will turn those mistakes to our advantage, since our intention is to have faith in Him.

To what extent can someone ask God's forgiveness for another person?
No one can intercede for anyone else unless God Himself gives them permission. In this story, only Benyâmin could do that.

THE STORY OF SHAYKH RASH

His name was Shaykh Rashîd, but because of the sin he committed it was changed to Shaykh Rash: *rash* means 'black' in Kurdish. His story is as follows:
There is a bridge on the river Sirvân that pilgrims had to

cross in order to reach the house of Hazrat-i Sultân. Since the road was dangerous, Sultân had placed a guard named Shaykh Rashîd at the other side of that bridge. One day a young woman among Sultân's disciples was crossing the bridge with her two children in order to bring Sultân the offering of a bowl of yoghurt, as she usually did almost every day. When Shaykh Rashîd saw that woman he was overcome by the desire to have her. When she rejected his advances he threatened to throw her two children into the river if she didn't give in to him. So when she continued to refuse, he threw over the first child and then the second. While this was happening some other people came along, and he was forced to let her by. The woman then came to Sultân, who asked her where were the children who usually accompanied her. She didn't reply. Then Sultân opened a door to his room and brought out the two children. At the instant when Shaykh Rashîd was throwing them into the river, Sultân had taken them and saved them through his spiritual power. That evening all the companions of Sultân held a spiritual gathering in his presence and Shaykh Rashîd also came in and sat down with the rest of them. Sultân wanted Rashîd to leave, but he didn't want to name him or say why, because he had the divine attribute of *al- Sattâr*, of the One who doesn't reveal the sins of others. So he ordered: 'Will he who has sinned leave our gathering!' Benyâmîn (one of his seven closest disciples) was the first to leave, immediately followed by the other *haftân*[6] and then by the rest of the disciples. The last one out was Shaykh Rashîd. Then Sultân cried out: 'Let the one who has sinned come back in!' Again Benyâmîn was the first, followed by the others and finally by shaykh Rashîd. Sultân ordered the sinners to leave another time, and the same scene was repeated three times, or seven times. Finally one of the other companions, Nariman, who was carrying his woodsman's axe, rushed toward Sultân in order to hit him with his axe. Sultân appeared to avoid his blow, and Nariman shouted: 'Why are you frightening us like this? Since you know everything, tell us who is the sinner!' Then Sultân said: 'Will Shaykh Rash leave.' They threw him outside, and his skin was immediately covered from head to toe with disgusting, foul-smelling abscesses, so that everyone fled whenever he came near. After a while Benyâmîn interceded on his behalf. Sultân said: 'In any case, I have excluded him from the Path of the Truth. But in order to be cured of this disease he has to eat the filthiest thing of all.' They asked him what that was, and he replied: the meat of a pig. So that was what happened: Shaykh Rash ate some pork and his disease was cured, but he was still banished from the Path of the Truth.

The key points to remember from this story are as follows:

1. Benyâmîn's attitude during the gathering. The purest disciples considered themselves the worst sinners.
2. The courage, faith and virtue of the young woman, who preferred to lose what the she held most dear, her own children, rather than to give in to sin.
3. The spiritual downfall of Shaykh Rash is a warning to us that we are always threatened by a revolt of our domineering self. There are three essential conditions for salvation: a true Master, the disciple's attachment to their Master, and the Connection.

   Here Shaykh Rash was, after all, a disciple of Sultân, and one with certain responsibilities. So we must only trust our Master; we shouldn't think that we are safe from our domineering self, or take on some particular attitude or form of behaviour because we think we're on the right path. And then you can see how one sin gives rise to another misdeed that we are forced to commit according to the law of action and reaction: after Shaykh Rash's sin he was obliged to eat pork, something forbidden.
4. As for Nariman's action, that was an impulse due to his complete faith in his Master, because Sultân's behaviour seemed to violate the original Agreement with God. If Sultân had to avoid his blow, that was because he was

vulnerable at that moment, since in principle the divine
Essence that he manifested could not be affected by it.
Why was it that way? What spiritual laws was Nariman
obeying when he attacked Sultân? According to the original Agreement, he demanded justice, he demanded
what was his legitimate right and the right of his companions; that is why Sultân was vulnerable. The others
hadn't done anything wrong, and Sultân had no right to
threaten them all because of the sins of a single individual.
God abides by His Agreement, and in this particular case
Nariman had the right to act as he did. It wasn't anger
that drove him to do it, but his faith: he was demanding
justice.

5. Why didn't Sultân indicate the guilty person right away?
This shows that God is always *al-Sattâr*, that He conceals
our sins rather than revealing them. Sultân was caught
between these two different attributes of God, but once
Nariman had attacked him he was obliged to reveal the
truth. For his disciples it was a terrible trial to be expelled;
they were afraid of God.

*How can a disciple be left to himself to the point that he comes to
do such horrible things?*

Such temptations can happen to all of us, but he should
have resisted and fought them by crying out for his Master's
help. His *nafs* was in a state of rebellion and that made him
forget Sultân. This person didn't have the spiritual capacity
to be one of Sultân's disciples; he didn't have the necessary
attachment to his Master. At least he should have gone to
Sultân and admitted his sin, he should have repented. But
instead he hid his wrongdoing until the very end. What kept
him from admitting it? It wasn't fear, since he wasn't afraid
to go to the spiritual gathering. It must have been pride, a
lack of attachment to his Master, and the absence of the
Connection. For if he had admitted his wrongdoing, Sultân
would surely have forgiven him. In principle, true spiritual
Masters arrange such scenes so that their students can learn

from them. This was a whole series of true scenes created by God. Each person was an actor, an integral part of this drama.

Can a person follow the path for years and then suddenly be excluded from it?

Yes, if that disciple breaks their Connection because of pride and disobedience. Keep telling yourself to be humble; continually pray for the divine Regard to stay with you and protect you against the domineering self and its allies. Don't always be saying 'me, me . . .': that's a sign of pride. The disciple who remains attached to their Master and doesn't break the Connection won't be excluded from the path.

V I

LIFE IN SOCIETY

Try to keep the same spiritual outlook no matter where you happen to be. Our behaviour should correspond to our spiritual personality, and we must keep in mind that God is always present in every situation. You don't need to proselytize for the spiritual path. In everyday life, at work, even with colleagues who are completely uninterested in spirituality, you must remember that you are a student of the path and that your behaviour should be in accord with your spiritual personality. Then you will avoid those words, actions and ways of behaving that would demean your spiritual character either outwardly or inwardly.

We shouldn't let ourselves be influenced by our social environment. Instead we ought to try to influence it: that's a spiritual exercise that will give excellent results.

I've tried that test myself. Before, when I was in my professional surroundings I forgot who I was and was caught up in that *milieu*. I spoke like my colleagues and made small talk like them; I pretended to agree with whatever they said, even when it was unseemly. But once I realized that I had to remain true to myself in whatever situation, I stopped participating in empty conversations, gossip, vulgar remarks and the like. It's very harmful for us to lose our identity in our surroundings and to be coloured by them. Instead, keep your own colour wherever you are, and then you will be transformed into light: for light keeps its own radiance and doesn't take on the colour of its surroundings. So try to keep the radiance of your own soul wherever you are, and then your colleagues, friends and family will no longer criticize your behaviour. I often hear that people complain about the behaviour of students in this school; and they're justified, because such students often have a disdainful, conceited attitude that comes from their not fully understanding the principles of their school.

So one day I came to a realization: I wasn't happy with my behaviour in the world outside my religious *milieu*, and I tried to figure out why. Finally I discovered the reason, and from then on I changed my inner outlook. I resist the influence of my surroundings and try to remain true to myself.

As long as we are gathered together here we have a proper way of acting and a spiritual way of thinking. Everything goes well because we have taken on the colour of our surroundings. But as soon as we leave here and find ourselves in contact with the rest of society we completely forget who we are. We forget that we have a different way of thinking, a different outlook, a different way of living and another path to travel, so that inwardly we cannot be like everyone else. You should keep a stable spiritual perspective. Try to be yourself and counterbalance the harmful influences of your surroundings. Keep your own inner character and outlook, because each person perceives and judges things accordingly. A person involved in politics sees everything from a political point of view, and a businessman views everything from an economic standpoint. So it's quite disturbing to note that while such people do keep their own particular personality, we completely forget our spiritual personality as soon as we find ourselves in materialistic surroundings and quickly take on their colour: if we're often around politicians we begin to speak like them; if we happen to be with people in high society we start to think like them; and if we're in an idle, frivolous *milieu* where people make fun of each other, then we do the same.

This doesn't mean we think we're better than others. We

respect their opinions, but we are following a different path. Their way is different from ours. When I say we must live in society, that means our outward, public comportment should be dignified, reasonable, respectable and responsible; we should influence those around us in the right direction and for the well-being of society, and we should resist the harmful influences of our surroundings on our inner personality. For example, when we accept a responsibility we should fulfil it conscientiously. We must respect the laws, and we should avoid any sort of freeloading, parasitic life, profligacy, extravagance, or any other deviations.

Is there a model of behaviour we should try to copy?
No. Try to be yourself. What is your way of thinking here, in this spiritual gathering? Then have the same inner outlook everywhere else. Be like others outwardly, but within yourself don't take on the colouring of your surroundings: if you live in Arabia, then wear a long robe; if you live in Europe, dress like Europeans do ... Or take another example: I don't like to wear a tie. In the past, if I didn't wear one everybody looked at me disapprovingly; my society considered that a tie was necessary then, so I had to wear one. But once the situation changed and most people no longer wore ties, I was among the first to stop. None of that has any importance: what really matters is the inner ground of our thought and intention.

Don't forget who you are. That is a purely inner task; people won't know how you think. If we're in a religious gathering we think right away that we should behave in a certain way, and we remember who we really are. But when we're elsewhere we very quickly forget and let ourselves be carried along by whatever is the current way of thinking. For example, not long ago everyone was caught up in politics; you talked about it all the time. Now if you had been true to yourselves you would have listened, and perhaps you would have discussed it, but you wouldn't have let yourselves be carried away.

Doesn't that mean wearing a mask all the time?

Not at all. I didn't say to wear a mask, but to be yourself. Only act that way with regard to certain aspects of social behaviour.

Work on it, and it will come to you gradually. I've taken fifteen years to reach this point. You should conduct yourself perfectly in public; for example, you should be a model of self-respect and diligence in your work. And you can only accomplish that if you don't forget who you are. If you're true to yourself you won't let your surroundings have a bad influence on you. Don't do things in order to please others; be yourself, whether that pleases them or not. You shouldn't be false and artificial, in one direction or the other. Being yourself means staying attentive to your spiritual self in all circumstances.

Sometimes you see people who behave so strangely . . .

And you'll notice that the fact that they're not dominated by their social *milieu* does attract a certain respect. Such individuals always have some sort of ideology, a distinctive way of thinking, because people without an ideology couldn't behave that way. They have a way of acting that is controlled by their basic way of thinking. You likewise have a comportment that is different from that of other people, and which is supported by arguments and solid principles. So you will be respectable if you put them into practice. But if, on the other hand, you only talk about the theory of the path, while your behaviour contradicts what you say, then people won't take you seriously. They will listen to your theories and find them excellent; but when they look at your behaviour they'll see that something's wrong and will pay no attention to you. For example, what if you say that politics is bad, but the next minute you're actively participating in political discussions? People will say that you've understood nothing, and that you're only following someone blindly. Many disciples are like that, especially those who want to proselytize and convert others.

What do you mean by the 'spiritual personality'?

That means being aware of your spiritual situation, of the special rank of your school and the responsibilities that you must take on in order to deserve to be the student of such a Master. Our spiritual personality is not yet fully formed. We are still evolving, and we don't yet have our fixed personality; it is more like that of a child who is changing and evolving from one instant to the next. However, during this evolution you can be in the state that is appropriate to your situation at each moment: try to be in that state, and remember who you are. We don't consider ourselves to be superior to other creatures, but we are the way we are. So we shouldn't forget our own specific way of thinking.

In all our surroundings and circumstances, remember that you should behave in such a way that people can't find fault with your actions. Of course they may not always agree with you, but they should consider you to be someone serious, sincere and self-respecting. When they notice that everything you do is logical and respectable then they'll begin to think that your ideas are also logical and coherent, even if they don't understand them. But if you act in a bizarre and irrational fashion even your best principles will be criticized.

You've talked about lying, but there are so many different kinds of lies that it's difficult to draw a general conclusion.

Lying is lying, and it's bad.

But there are several ways to lie: you can make up something that isn't so, you can lie by not telling the whole story, or you can exaggerate or phrase things in such a way that the other person understands something other than the truth.

A person must be honest and upright – that is, not lie – except for certain special situations: there are lies which, without harming anyone, can save lives and avoid a catastrophe. But obviously this doesn't mean that you should, for example, go around revealing the intimate secrets of your private life to total strangers . . .

Does lying mean intending to mislead someone?
Yes, or to harm or wrong them. For example, a husband and wife must absolutely never lie to one another, without any exception.

Even if that could hurt the other person?
If you get used to not lying, then you will not do anything that could hurt the other person. This attitude brings a special spiritual blessing (*barakat*) to their home.

But distorting the truth, or exaggerating it – don't you consider that to be a form of lying?
To distort or misrepresent spiritual and religious truths is a deadly sin. Exaggeration, like clouds, obscures the Truth and lessens its powers of penetration, and can even completely block its radiance.

Someone commits themself to a business transaction and then changes their mind: should we consider them to have broken their word?
That depends on the contract and the situation in general. But someone who is a believer must keep their promises; or else they must get the other person to let them out of their agreement.

When people ask us about our religious beliefs there are situations where we have to be quite straightforward and say what we think, but there are other cases where we have the impression that it isn't worth it. Is there any rule on how to respond?
That depends on the receptiveness of the person you're talking with and the particular situation. In situations where a person's life, honour and reputation are at stake they do have the right to conceal their belief; but if they don't do so that is considered an act of self-sacrifice for God's sake.

Then what should we say?

Generalities, the sort of generalities that are accepted everywhere.

Some people lie because of mental problems – I mean they automatically have mistaken notions about certain things.

If they follow the path and work at it, then in principle that sort of problem should gradually disappear. When we say not to lie that also means we shouldn't lie to ourselves, shouldn't fool ourselves. Most people deceive themselves. We shouldn't lie at all, in any respect. But of course you have to adapt what you say to each particular situation. You have to speak one way with little children, another way with people you don't know, a different way with your close acquaintances, with colleagues, or with your wife, and so on. It depends; you have to adapt yourself to all sorts of circumstances. One can't give a simple formula, to say that it ought to be like this or like that. The rule is to tell the same truth, but to phrase it appropriately according to the person you're addressing.

But can't we find an approach that would be the same in every case?

No, that isn't possible; you have to adapt yourself to the particular people, society and circumstances at hand. People aren't all alike, so you can't have the same formula for everybody. But the basic principle is that you have to be sincere with yourself: if you are genuinely sincere with yourself and you hate to lie, then you will find the appropriate way. Sometimes you may feel obligated to lie, for example in order to avoid serious disturbances, a catastrophe, and things like that.

But doesn't being perfectly sincere with yourself mean not having any more psychological problems and truly knowing yourself?

If you are genuinely sincere with yourself you will be

sincere with others. This is a step towards true knowledge of the self.

How should we respond to people we know are lying? Should we tell them we know they're lying to us?

No. As soon as you know they're lying you no longer trust them and they can't fool you any longer. One of the people who comes here was a technician at the airport a number of years ago. One night when he was on duty, he got into an army jeep without permission and crashed into the private aeroplane of a prominent figure. And that was at a time when everyone was very afraid. So he went to the Master to ask what he should do, and the Master told him not to lie. The next day they began to question everyone, and he came forward to say he was the guilty party. They didn't believe him; they thought he was crazy, or just simple. But finally he proved he really was guilty – and they forgave him and actually gave him a reward for being so honest! Now ever since then he has been known to be a man who doesn't lie. Whenever something happens they go to him to find out the true story. But if he hadn't asked the Master he surely would have lied.

When someone lives in a society and profits from its benefits they must obey the laws of that society. If you don't obey a society's laws you are creating disorder in it. You shouldn't disobey the laws unless you are not living in society at all – and someone who doesn't live in society is being selfish and irresponsible. Society is our training ground, our laboratory. If we leave our laboratory behind to go and live as a hermit, how can we practise and try out what we've learned? Those who withdraw from society are like people living in a sterilized environment without any germs: they're imprisoned by their own situation, because as soon as they leave and come into contact with the outside world they fall sick and die. But those who live in society gradually become vaccinated. They eventually reach a state in which they can live in any surroundings. So when you compare them, which is superior to the other? The person who is vaccinated and resistant to anything, or the one who can't leave their sterilized environment? The longer you live in a polluted environment the stronger you become. And it's the same from the point of view of spirituality. The person who withdraws from society and lives as a hermit runs the risk of losing everything in their first real contact with temptation.

Isn't it normal to withdraw from society at a certain age?

No, you shouldn't withdraw from society but you do have to reduce your level of activity, because old age doesn't allow you to be as active. However you should still be as active as your strength allows. That is why every form of study, material as well as spiritual, should begin during one's youth, except for certain exceptional cases. The soul doesn't get old, but the body does. That is why the soul, which always has the same energy for working, should take advantage of the young and enthusiastic body that is available to it at the start. For after a while, when you get old and your body has lost its strength, the soul is riding a feeble steed.

Isn't that offset by the greater strength of the soul itself?

Yes, the soul may be stronger, but do you think that an older person doesn't have a *nafs* that is just as strong? Older people are worse than young ones in that regard. If you fight against your *nafs* when you're young it will be weaker when you get old. But if you don't fight it, it only changes form and manifests itself differently, but without becoming any weaker. When you're young your *nafs* manifests itself in the form of passion and carnal desire, but as you get older it takes on the forms of pride, conceit, greed and envy, which are worse. Just as the soul doesn't age, neither does the *nafs*; its destructive power doesn't weaken with age. But if you succeed in overcoming your *nafs* when you're young you will still dominate it when it changes form as you get older. You can advance spiritually until you die, and even beyond.

A human being is like a cutting planted in the ground: the more impurities there are in the soil, the more fertile it is; so the faster the plant grows, if it is well taken care of. Our surroundings now are excellent, full of fertilizer. So we need to work with them.

Shouldn't we try to improve society? Isn't it our duty to do so?

Society is made up of individuals; if all those individuals try to correct themselves the society will also be improved. It's your duty to correct your own surroundings, to improve society to the extent that concerns you. What concerns you, first of all, is to try to correct yourself; then you are fulfilling your duty. God doesn't ask any more of us, and we can't do any more than that. When He wants to undertake something more He sends an emissary on His behalf who has the mission of correcting society. But as for us, we don't have the power to go beyond the limits of our duty.

It is difficult for us, too, to adapt ourselves to this society. But the more the soul dominates the body the better we are able to keep our equilibrium. Society today is entirely dedicated to the well-being of the body, and people forget the fact that there are two dimensions in us: the dimension of the *nafs* (the carnal soul) and that of the angelic soul. Those who have never tried to go beyond their *basharic* dimension, who are dominated by their *nafs*, are quite at home in this society. But as soon as a person becomes aware of that other, spiritual dimension it becomes hard for them to adapt. This life becomes difficult for them; they sense that this is not their true homeland, their own *milieu*, that this is not their eternal home, and they feel like a stranger here. The proof of this is that they're not afraid of death, whereas other people are extremely attached to earthly life. When you become aware of that other dimension you understand better why our Master said: 'Act in such a way that you don't come back again.' But other people are very satisfied with their situation here. We don't claim to be better than them; we're only explaining our own perceptions.

How can you reconcile the notion that this world is lowly and despicable with the idea in the Qur'an that simply through contemplating the universe we can see God's handiwork?

In the Qur'an God's words are directed to those who worshipped the sun, moon and the stars and who denied the existence of the One God. Look at the earth, nature, the planets, and the rest: Who created them, if it wasn't the Creator? But if you are sensitive only to the beauty of nature it's because you haven't looked any higher than that. People in their human-animal, *basharic* state only think of eating, sleeping, sex, and so on. But for us this world in comparison to the other world is like a sort of purgatory or whatever you want to call it. However at the same time it is also our school. So we should follow our lessons and study, because this is the place where we can learn and advance.

Should a person avoid withdrawing from the world or living in special communities far from cities and towns?

I haven't had the experience of living in a small artificial community; our school doesn't approve of leading a life separated from society. The Master says that society is an inexhaustible source of spiritual trials which allows the student who passes those tests to advance in the path of perfection.

What are the duties of a student of the path of perfection with regard to money, material and spiritual success, material and spiritual rank, or ambition?

Students of the path can obtain and use such things as long as they do so legally and in a religiously licit fashion. But they must avoid greed for material things, and try to use their possessions judiciously and appropriately. They can have worldly goods, but if they're a genuine student of this school they'll know the intrinsic value of each thing – that is, they won't be the slave of their possessions. Do you see the difference? What is different is that people are often enslaved by what they own. As for the disciples of this path, they can have those goods but they mustn't become controlled by them or attached to them.

In everyday life a person sometimes has to be aggressive. Can someone be completely humble and at the same time still defend their own rights?

The person who is in a state of true humility also defends himself, but only because it is his duty. Because he acts calmly and carefully he can pretend to be aggressive. He tells himself: 'Here it is my duty to defend my rights; but in that case I don't have the duty to defend myself.' Moreover, what other people think isn't very important; their opinion is no longer a problem for such a truly humble person. You see, our big problem is 'other people'. If you can manage to get them out of your mind you can really be yourself.

Try to understand what I mean: we have a duty toward ourselves and a duty toward others. When you're hungry you have to eat. Even in religion, when they tell you that if you have some food you can give it as charity, that means you can give your food away to the extent that doing so doesn't harm you. Our duty is first of all toward our soul; then come our spouse and children, then our parents, other relatives, neighbours, our community, and so on. This is what God and the Prophet have said.

Why is that?

The reason is: What is our duty here on earth? Why have we come here?

But isn't it written that we should help our neighbour and serve others?

Of course you ought to help your neighbour, but you have to be able to do so. If someone doesn't have any arms, for example, how can they help someone else? You have to have strong arms indeed in order to be able to help someone who doesn't have any. Even with regard to religion, try to form your own self properly so that you'll be able to help others. Because whatever you can do for other people is only through your self.

But what other limits are there, beyond that?
I don't desire anything beyond what is necessary. But if God grants it to me I accept it.

What about the example of Ali and Fatima, who fasted for three days because they gave their meal to a poor person for three days in a row?
Although that was an exemplary act of sacrifice, they also didn't do any harm to their bodies. And in fact we now know that it's excellent for your health to fast for three days each month. I believe that in some Christian groups as well they also have one day a week of fasting, or at least of partial abstinence. One day of fasting a week, or three days a month, is very good for your health.

Of total fasting?
There is a total fast of three days, and if it is spiritually guided it gives excellent results. But if it is not done under the guidance of an authentic Master it can have disastrous spiritual consequences.

What is the spiritual situation of people who have devoted their whole life to the service of humankind: scientists, doctors, researchers, and so forth?
They are judged according to their intentions. If their intention from the very start was to serve others that is excellent. However, science itself is extremely tempting. When you become involved in it you forget everything else, and you only want to live in your laboratory. You may think that you are working to help others when in reality you are still only living for yourself. Truly 'living for others'

is for the person who has reached the end of 'living for one's self'; that is, the person who has completed that spiritual stage. From then on they can genuinely live for others; but before that it's impossible. However if a person makes discoveries that are useful for mankind, even if they were only aiming to satisfy themselves, that is still excellent. They are judged according to their intentions and also according to the consequences of their discoveries.

Yet such people have often been the least religious and the least mystical.

Yes, but we are all religious whether we think so or not. Even an avowed materialist is religious, except that he's changed the terms; he's playing with words. If we ask him he says: 'I don't believe in God, I believe in my conscience.' What we call 'God' he calls 'conscience', because the conscience flows from the angelic soul, and the angelic soul takes its life from the divine particle within each of us.

We need to distinguish between the official religions – for example, the one into which we are born – and authentic, real religion, the divine religion God has sent down with His own prophets: the pure religion. Everyone inwardly believes in that pure religion; it is the true, authentic religion. The official religions have been transformed into philosophic or social ideologies, and many people don't believe in them. But the true religion is within each of us, and we do believe in it. Even those individuals you just mentioned are really very good and decent people inside. It's unimportant whether or not they have an official religion: they act like religious people, and it's our behaviour, our spiritual comportment, that matters. Our conscience is God's echo within us, and the person who acts according to their conscience is in contact with God. What is religion, after all? It's to establish a relationship with God in order to come to know Him.

To come back to the question about what sort of standard of living is necessary, what are the limits beyond which we shouldn't go, in either direction?

Those limits depend on the social position of the individual. For example the Islamic religion says that an engineer, a doctor, a learned person, or someone else with a genuinely superior social position ought to have the kind of life that is in keeping with their social status. That is a religious law. The 'classless society' is unattainable in practice. It's like the expression 'dove of peace': someone made it up, but people still continue to slaughter one another in the name of peace. In the Qur'an there's a verse that says: 'I created you, and I gave some of you an advantage over others.'

And yet in China there really are managers who earn the same wages as their workers.

Yes, but I'm talking about the intrinsic worth of a person, not the kind of status someone bestows with a few words written on a piece of paper and then takes away from you with another piece of paper. That intrinsic value is given by God: for example, a saint, someone with a particular artistic talent, an excellent doctor, an inventor . . .

Each of us should live according to his or her situation. For example, when I was a student I had nothing, and for one month I slept on the floor. After that when I wanted to lie down in a bed I wasn't able to get to sleep; so I got out and lay down on the floor and then I slept quite soundly.

The truth lies in being satisfied with your state, in being happy and satisfied with it. That's an inner state, a particular sensation. Take another example: say you have a baby with a mother who is ugly, dirty and poor, and you separate him from his mother so that you can make him live in a palace. Which is he going to prefer, his mother's breast or the palace? We may think the palace is great, but for that child his own mother is best.

Therefore well-being in life doesn't depend on the sort of outward conditions we believe to be so important. For example, don't imagine that someone who lives in a poor neighbourhood is more unhappy than another person who lives in a rich area. I don't mean there aren't any exceptions among these two groups, but if they live in surroundings where there is no injustice and favouritism they will feel at ease. But if they feel they are suffering from injustice they will be unhappy wherever they are. Therefore you should strive to eliminate injustice from society, and in that case everyone will be happy. Take the case of a carpenter: if he likes his work, if there is no injustice, and if he knows that all the other carpenters of his rank live in the same way, then he's a very happy person.

If you can manage to decrease social injustice everyone will be happy. Eliminate social injustice and lying; give each person what they deserve. But giving everyone the same thing is impossible and unjust, because we aren't all alike, we don't have the same tastes, desires and abilities. Even the fingerprints of any two individuals are not alike, so why should we imagine that their minds and temperaments should be the same? We aren't like sheep, so that you could say everyone should live the same way. That's impossible, which is why I say it's a myth.

Jesus said that we shouldn't become attached to material goods.

Yes, it was Jesus who said that. 'Not to be attached' means not to have a weakness for material things, not to let material questions preoccupy us to the point that we forget about spirituality. We mustn't let material things become our ultimate goal, whether in the sense of trying to possess a great deal or of trying not to own anything at all. This sort of detachment is only a means, and being inwardly detached from things is quite different from not possessing anything. This is an absolutely fundamental point in the spiritual path. For example, I'm not attached to this carpet, but I do own it now; I won't throw it out, because I need it. It's not something superfluous in my life, not a useless luxury, since I'm sitting on it. But I'm not attached to it; if a thief were to walk off with it that wouldn't change anything for me.

As long as we possess an object we can enjoy it, since God gave it to us. As long as I possess something it is also my obligation to appreciate it and to use it. We shouldn't scorn material goods or any other created thing: every created thing has its own reason for existing, its own justification and proper use, and a certain influence on other created things. Things are only harmful if we use them wrongly and inappropriately. It is not creation that is bad, but rather our misuse and abuse of things which brings about evil consequences. Instead of judging creation, we ought to judge ourselves.

Do you mean we ought to be satisfied with possessing only what is necessary?

We must have everything that is necessary, but what is 'necessary' differs according to each individual's position in society. For example, the dean of a faculty has different needs to a doorman. What is necessary varies, and each person should have what is in keeping with their situation. All that depends on the particular society in which a person lives. People today who withdraw from the world with the pretence of being 'detached' from everything don't inspire me with trust. Study them up close and you'll see what I mean . . . Of course there are always people who simply like to live alone, and who don't claim to be detached from things.

A rich young man asked Jesus: 'What should I do in order to reach the Kingdom of Heaven?' And Jesus answered him: 'Give everything you own to the poor.'

That prescription was correct, but only for the particular young man in question; it was not meant to be extended to everybody. When those who have reached perfection give an order to someone that doesn't mean the same order is valid for everyone. On the path of perfection each order and each precept are different for each individual. For example, if you ask the Master: 'How should I act in this situation?', he will advise you to do this or that. But if you ask him the same thing later he will give you a different answer. And if you ask him yet again, perhaps he will say something else. Therefore, when Jesus gave an order at a given time, to a particular person in a specific spiritual state, that can't be taken as a universal rule. It's quite possible that this same young man could ask that question at another time and that he would be told to keep his possessions. People are mistaken if they think that when a prophet gives an order to someone that order applies to everyone and for all time. That's false. You will never find two people on earth with exactly the same mental and spiritual states. And since their minds and thoughts are not alike, the orders and prescriptions they require are also different.

When the Master was with several people and each of them asked him the same question about the same subject, he would give each of them a different reply according to their spiritual state at that moment. A true Master is like a spiritual doctor, and we are like patients. If two patients both have a fever the doctor will give each of them a different prescription: he may tell one not to eat and the other to eat a great deal. Which one is right? In fact they both are: one of them should eat, and the other one shouldn't. And of course these orders aren't forever. As soon as God has changed someone's spiritual state, that person will need a new rule, a new prescription. An authentic Master is like that: he looks at the soul of each person and gives them the prescription that is required by the particular state of their soul.

People who know nothing about spirituality are unaware of these principles. Their clergy tell them that a prophet said this or that – but everything depends on the person that prophet was addressing. Of course there are also general principles for the exoteric side of religion that are valid for everyone: for example, that you should only worship a single unique God, that you shouldn't kill, nor lie, nor violate the rights of others, and so forth. But beyond that stage, at the stage of the traveller on the spiritual path, each rule and each precept concerns a particular group. And when you reach the stage of the 'spiritual university' each individual must receive their own specific orders and pre-scriptions.

If we feel uncomfortable in the luxurious surroundings in which we were born, should we look for a simpler sort of life?

If you yourself went out seeking luxury, then that isn't good. But if God wished to give you that luxury, neither should you simply reject it so that you can say 'I'm unpre-tentious.' You can make use of your possessions without letting them dominate you. Ali led a simple life in order to set an example for others. When he was caliph he wanted to live like the poorest person of his realm, because he felt responsible for the condition of his subjects. That was Ali's political justice: he put himself in the place of the poorest of his subjects in order to understand them.

The outward conduct of each of God's messengers or saints is in accordance with their own time and circum-stances. I don't believe that in our own day it would be appropriate to live materially like the saints at the very beginning of Islam, since the times have changed. On the other hand, we should always keep in mind the example of their spiritual life.

Why do the disciples have the right to get married, but not to have relations with whomever they want?

Because otherwise this wouldn't be a spiritual gathering, but a meeting of animals. And in some schools that's exactly what happens . . . The students in the school of the Master should be pure and decent.

The customs are different in Europe; you choose your own husband or wife, and you get to know each other well before you get married. But in Iran it's the parents who choose, so you don't know who it is you're marrying.

There's no problem with that. Between men and women in Europe there is always this deception which consists in saying you can't get married unless you've first known each other well. I haven't noticed that European marriages are any more successful than those in the East. Marriage is like a roll of the dice: whether in Europe or elsewhere, it's the same thing . . . And yet Islamic marriages seem more successful than European ones. In Europe girls are often young and follow their feelings rather than reason, so they frequently make mistakes. In fact, marriage is a sort of 'commercial' problem, a contract: whether you're a man or a woman, you should approach marriage with all the good judgement and practical wisdom of an experienced businessperson. You have to try not to be cheated, to make your choice clearheadedly and objectively, without following your passions, since passion blinds your good sense and better judgement. I don't believe in marriage 'for love'; that's another slogan. Needless to say, sympathy and mutual attraction do play a role; if you don't have any sympathy or attraction for someone then you can't marry them.

What points should you take into consideration in the other person before you get married?
You have to look at their life from every conceivable perspective: their family, education, behaviour, intelligence, physique, social situation, points you have in common, and so forth. The woman should especially consider whether the man is someone who will stay with her for life. All too often girls prefer a Prince Charming, a Don Juan who frequently turns out to be good for nothing. Really serious men, those ready for a lifetime together, are rarely the most dashing suitors. But when a marriage is based on rational considerations the couple very seldom turn out to be incompatible. Gradually a feeling of friendship, affection and attraction develops and grows up between them, and they will become solidly bound together, on the condition that they don't lie to each other. The 'great love', 'love at first sight',

are fine for adolescents. But then they should get married. It's better to get married young: the less 'experience' you have the better. This argument for 'experience' was invented by men in order to take advantage of women; it's a lie and deception.

What should one do when a couple starts to argue and fight?
If other people stay out of it they'll make peace and get along together again. You have to leave them alone; after a while, in the nature of things, they'll gradually get along again. But if other people get involved, then they'll find it hard to come to agreement. You should always try to avoid arguments with your spouse; even if the other person is wrong, that doesn't matter. Between husband and wife you shouldn't try to figure out who is right or wrong, because they are really only one. You shouldn't wait for the other person to apologize; no, the main thing is to get rid of that state of dissension. This is extremely important in our spiritual life. You can try to convince the other person; but after a while one of you makes peace and the argument's over. If you start reasoning about it, trying to make your point of view understood, you risk getting involved in an argument. But if you wait that state will pass.

Can a couple choose not to have children?
Yes, on condition that they're both in agreement about that. However if one of them doesn't agree, then that person has to convince the other. The same thing is true for deciding the number of children; they have to come to a mutual understanding.

Some people think you should live alone and not pay any attention to what your parents say even when you are still very young. Is that right?
No it's not. That's just something they made up. Even simple logic denies that, since parents love their children in an unbiased way and have had more experience of life. In

the East they say that parents are always right, and that you should obey them until the end of your days. In the West they say the opposite. But both views are false. I simply say that you should respect them and take into account what they say.

Children should follow their parents as long as their own intelligence and knowledge are not sufficiently developed, and after that they should try to find the Truth and seek it on their own. As soon as someone has the faculty of discernment it is their duty to seek the Truth and find out whether what their society says is really the truth or not.

What do you do when you become ill?

When I'm sick I take care of myself just like everyone else, since I have a duty towards my body. I go to see the doctor, and I follow his orders. But deep down within myself I don't worry how things may turn out; I submit to God's will. That is, if the doctors manage to cure me I'll thank God and I'll say that it was really God who healed me, because I consider the doctors and medicines to be only a means. And if I'm not cured I'll likewise thank God and submit to His will. Since He didn't want to heal me, the doctors and their means were ineffective.

Do you see the difference between us and a materialist? A materialist believes that the doctors and medicines were the only active cause and, as it were, the ultimate cause; he leaves out God's will, as though everything came down to the doctors and medicine. But I consider the doctors and their treatments simply as certain means among others, since I've sometimes seen God heal without them, for example through a written phrase, a piece of bread or something else that had been blessed. I've seen gravely ill people cured of their sickness after they had been given something that was blessed. So after I had seen that I realized that the One who Heals and bestows illnesses is someone other than the doctors. But that same being, who is God, has put those means at our disposal, so it is our duty to respect the law of ultimate cause–means–effect and to have ourselves treated like everyone else, although without worrying about the final outcome. Indeed if God wants to take someone away then no doctor can save them, even if that person has available all the means in the world. Some day science will be able to treat all the diseases, do away with ageing and prolong our lifespan, but it will never be able to stop death.

Should we vote? Doesn't that sometimes mean voting for negative forces?

Voting doesn't mean becoming a politician; it's our social duty. However you should vote for someone you're convinced will work for the good of society.

And what about becoming a soldier?

There's no harm in being a soldier. The law tells you to obey your officers, so you obey them. In any case you must obey the law of your country.

But if a soldier is participating in an unjust war?

That's a social matter, not a spiritual one. A solider, by definition, must obey the orders of his officers; that doesn't mean he becomes a politician. We shouldn't get involved in politics, but military service is legally mandatory. If they send us to war we'll go to war. You see, that doesn't concern our path; it's something that's imposed on us by society. So we obey because we respect the laws, that's all.

But war, in any case, is never just.

No, sometimes it's clear that a war is just. For example, in the past, when one tribe was attacked by another tribe; then you knew it was just to resist. But nowadays nobody knows whether a war is just, or even who really started it. We're in a state of complete chaos, so our personal judgement can't decide ... One person insists that a war is just, while someone else assures us that it's unjust. And when you get down to the bottom of the story you see that no one really knows who's behind it all. It was simply the personal interests of a few individuals at stake, and they started the war in the name of their country.

What attitude should we have in society with regard to all the various verbal and physical acts of aggression that come from others?

You should defend your rights. You can pardon someone who violates your own rights, but not someone who attacks the rights of others. For example, if someone at work spreads rumours about you, then you're entitled to defend your personal reputation and to make the truth known. Once you've done that, whether people believe you or not is unimportant; you've done your duty. In general it's not worth insisting too much on your rights when that will have no real effect.

If you're harmed by someone else (in an accident, or things like that) you can receive damages. But some people think an accident is sent by God, so that you shouldn't ask the other person for damages: if you were destined to lose that money and manage to get it back from the other person, then you'll only lose it some other way. You are free to take the damages or not. In Islamic law you have the right to ask for damages. For example, if you've lent money to someone and you see that they would like to pay you back but can't, then you shouldn't force them to repay you. On the other hand, if you see that the person has the money but is simply unwilling to repay you, then you should take them to court.

But sometimes you have to spend a great deal of energy defending your rights when the matter at stake isn't really worth it.

You are obligated to expend your energy in order to uphold the law and ensure the rule of justice and right. That is your duty, even when it means spending a thousand dollars in order to gain ten in damages. That is also the religious law. You may lose money, but society wins as a result. We ought to try to help establish and uphold the social law. (One of the missions of the prophets was to ensure the rule of justice in society, even at the risk of their lives.) That may seem unreasonable, but the consequences are extremely important. If everyone did the same thing there would be no more swindlers. In doing so we make sure that the law is respected in our society and we follow the precepts of the path.

That is what is so difficult: sometimes you have to be as hard as stone, and sometimes you have to be very soft and yielding. With ill-intentioned people you must continue until they're actually punished; and then it's finished. You shouldn't be aggressive, but you do have to uphold the law and let people know it exists. If you aren't motivated by hatred you will stay calm and self-possessed, and then you will stop as soon as your opponent has sufficiently learned his lesson.

Should you intervene, for example, if you surprise a thief in the act of stealing something?

You need to know whether it's your mission to arrest thieves; and if you're not sure the person is a thief that isn't your business. But if you know that they're a thief, then help ensure the security of your society.

It's difficulty to imagine that someone could carry on a lawsuit or defend their rights without the intrusion of any spirit of revenge, hatred or aggressiveness.

If you are dealing with a 'humanoid', a human-animal, and your only defence lies in fighting that person, then you must act like them if you can. But even in such an extreme case you should always act in a spirit of self-defence, never with aggressiveness. We must only be aggressive in attacking our own domineering self; apart from that, our attitude should only be to defend ourselves.

If it is impossible for us to settle some of our debts on the material plane, can we satisfy them by praying for those who have rightful claims against us?

That depends on the debts in question. There are two kinds of debts: the ones that are called *Haqq an-nâs*, that is, our debts toward other people; and our debts to God, *haqq Allâh*. As for our debts toward others we have to repay them, either in this world or in the other world. And of course it's much better to settle them in this world, since otherwise you'll be obliged to repay them in the other world. The only exception is for those who sincerely intend to satisfy their debts but don't have the means to do so. God will repay those debts for them; true repentance removes the *haqq an-nâs*.

If someone has stolen, lied and trampled on the rights of others, what must that person do in order to make amends for that?

If that person truly repents, becoming an upright individual from every point of view, believing and practising religion, then God will help them a great deal, whether in this world or in the other world.

Christians believe that repentance automatically erases our sins, and that you only have to pray sincerely to God in order to be forgiven.

As for our sins against others (*haqq an-nâs*), no; God doesn't automatically forgive them. He says: 'I will not forgive the *haqq an-nâs*.' That is to say, where the harm we've done to other people is concerned, it is up to them to forgive us. But if we've sinned against God (what is called *haqq Allâh*), then our repentance is accepted. Don't forget that when someone continues to repent until the end of their life God will come to their aid and will save them even if other people have a claim against them. But this doesn't mean He forgives that offence against others; you need to understand that distinction.

What about people who take drugs, commit perverted acts, and so forth, but who afterwards repent and are forgiven: must they still suffer the consequences of those actions?

They have to undergo their bodily consequences, although those effects gradually disappear. Sins have two sorts of consequences: an immediate outcome or reaction; and their ultimate results, either in this world or, more commonly, in the other world.

It's important to understand the difference between *haqq Allâh* and *haqq an-nâs*. The sins and acts of disobedience you have committed with respect to God are called *haqq Allâh*. For example, in the religion of Judaism God has forbidden working on the Sabbath or eating pork, and He has ordered certain fasts. So if someone following that religion eats pork they've committed a sin. And if they repent of those sins God will pardon them.

But *Haqq an-nâs*, for example, is things like borrowing money and not repaying it, or harming someone who didn't deserve it. When a married woman deceives her husband she has committed the sin of adultery (a case of *haqq Allâh*) and at the same time she has incurred a situation of *haqq an-nâs* with regard to her husband. If she repents God will forgive her act of adultery, but her husband must also forgive her for it. The particular moral 'accounts' of unmarried men and women with regard to *haqq an-nâs* depend on the conventions of their society.

Nothing of what is written in this book is mine. These are my Master's lessons. All these discoveries are his, and I have only repeated what I have heard from him and what I have tried to practise myself to the limited extent of my abilities.

May God forgive me if I have not succeeded in serving that cause.

The way through this dense forest of the path of perfection has been traced by the Master, and we can do no more than follow him.

NOTES

PREFACE

1. *Burhân al Haqq* (*Demonstration of the Truth*), Tehran, 1979; *Ma'rifat al-Rûh* (*Knowing the Soul*), Tehran, 1969; *Hâshiya bar Haqq al-Haqâ'iq* (Commentary on *The Truth of Truths*), Tehran, 1985.
2. *Athâr al-Haqq* (*Traces of the Truth*), Tehran, 1979.
3. Element Books, Shaftesbury, 1993; originally published as *La Voie de la perfection*, Albin Michel, Paris, 1982 (2nd edition).

INTRODUCTION

1. See *The Path of Perfection*, Chapters 30 and 31.
2. Nur Ali Elahi's sister, who continues to lead a life of spiritual retreat in her native village of Jayhunabad, in Iranian Kurdistan.

CHAPTER 1

1. One of the greatest Iranian philosophers and scientists (d. 1037).
2. Or motion 'in place' (*vaz'î*), as contrasted with the ordinary soul's linear movement (*intiqâl*) of spiritual advancement – or regression – from one level to another.

3. Bahram Elahi, *The Path of Perfection*, Element Books, Shaftesbury, 1993; French edition: Albin Michel, Paris, 1982.
4. *Kayfiyat*: a unique state or distinctive quality that can only be experienced, that can't be communicated by words alone.
5. *The Path of Perfection*, (Chapter 8).
6. That is, those qualities or characteristics belonging to people insofar as they compose part of the human-animal (*bashar*), as distinct from the angelic soul.
7. The 'voyager' on the spiritual path, the spiritual disciple.
8. The Umayyad caliph indirectly responsible for the martyrdom of the Imam Husayn (son of the Imam Ali and grandson of the Prophet Muhammad) at Kerbala.

CHAPTER 2

1. *Sharî'at*: an exoteric religious code or law.
2. *Valî*: God's 'viceroy' on earth, who exists in every age; the *Valî* is a perfect human being who reflects the divine Essence.
3. A reference to the martyrdom of Husayn Ibn Ali, grandson of the Prophet Muhammad, along with many of his close relatives and followers, at Kerbala on the 10th of Muharram, 61 AH, after he had been surrounded by much larger forces loyal to the Umayyad caliph Yazîd.
4. A two-stringed lute (to which Nur Ali added a third string) played in the spiritual gatherings of certain mystical orders in Kurdistan. Master Elahi was an incomparable player of this instrument, for which he created a spiritual repertoire including earlier sacred music, traditional melodies and his own original compositions.
5. At the end of Chapter 1 above.
6. *Ali* ('the Sublime', 'the Exalted'): one of the Names of God.

CHAPTER 3

1. *Hujjat*: argument, reasoning, proof. The *itmâm hujjat* is a decisive and incontrovertible proof, one that cannot be questioned.
2. *Sharî'at, tarîqat, ma'rifat*, and *Haqîqat* are the four spiritual stages, corresponding to the exoteric aspect of religion, the spiritual Path, mystical understanding, and the Truth. (See *The Path of Perfection* Chapter 31.)

CHAPTER 4

1. *Zikr*, in this context, refers to the collective sessions of vocal prayer and chanting, sometimes accompanied by music or percussion, commonly practised by many spiritual groups in Islam.
2. Hajji Ni'matullah (1873–1920), the father of Nur Ali Elahi.
3. The spiritual maturity someone has acquired during their preceding lives remains engraved in that person's soul; often they'll only become aware of it during a spiritual trial.
4. *Valî*: God's 'viceroy' on earth, who exists in every age; the *Valî* is a perfect human being who reflects the divine Essence.
5. See *The Path of Perfection*, Chapters 34–36.
6. Literally, the 'left-handed way'; *râstlari* is the 'right-handed way'.

CHAPTER 5

1. Qur'an 40:60.
2. *Athâr al-Haqq* (*The Traces of the Truth*), Tehran, 1977: Chapter 24, saying no. 1914.
3. *The Path of Perfection*, Chapter 38.
4. Nur Ali's sister, who was born in 1906 in Jayhunabad, the village in Kurdistan where she continues to lead a life of spiritual retreat and detachment from the world.
5. Sultân Ishaq, the founder of the spiritual order of the Ahl-i Haqq ('those devoted to God') in fourteenth-century Kurdistan.
6. 'The seven' individuals who were Sultân's most intimate disciples and companions.

GLOSSARY

Ahl-i Haqq   'Followers of the Truth', or those devoted to God (*al Haqq*), belonging to an esoteric spiritual order established by Sultân Ishaq in the fourteenth century (see *The Path of Perfection*, Chapter 39).

Ali   The first Imam (in Shiite Islam), the Prophet's cousin and son-in-law, a manifestation of the divine Essence.

barzakh   The intermediate world of the soul, between the material world and the eternal world.

bashar, basharic   The human-animal, or people considered as belonging to the human species, without regard to their spiritual dimension; the *basharic* soul is the soul of the human-animal.

chaplarî   A particular type of spiritual method (see Chapter 4).

ghaflat   Unconsciousness, ignorance, or heedlessness in the spiritual path.

Haqîqat   The Truth, the True Reality: the final stage of spirituality in which the disciple reaches the goal of perfection and reunion with God.

Haqq (al-Haqq)   God, the Truth, Reality (one of the Names of God); what is right, just; what is deserved, one's due.

haqq Allâh   'God's due', our duties and obligations toward God.

Haqq an-nâs   'What is owed to other people', our obligations toward our fellow human beings and all other creatures.

Husayn	The third Shiite Imam, son of Ali and grandson of the Prophet, who died as a martyr at Kerbala (61 AH/680 CE).
Imâm	Title reserved in Shiism for Ali and his eleven descendants who were entrusted with mystical understanding (*ma'rifat*) in Islam.
itmâm hujjat	Ultimate argument or decisive proof, which leaves no possibility of complaint or appeal.
ma'rifat	Spiritual knowledge or understanding; the stage of mystical gnosis (preceding *Haqîqat*).
mazharullâh	A theophany, someone (or something) who manifests the divine Essence.
nafs	The domineering self (an abbreviated expression for *nafs-i ammâra*, 'the self commanding evil' mentioned in the Qur'an, 12:53).
râstlarî	A particular type of spiritual method (see Chapter 4).
rûh	The angelic soul (an abbreviated form of *rûh-i malakûtî*, the 'angelic spirit').
Sultân Ishaq	The founder of the spiritual order of the Ahl-i Haqq in fourteenth-century Kurdistan.
sharî'at	The law or exoteric dimension of each authentic religion; the spiritual stage of exotericism, preceding *tarîqat*.
tarîqat	'The Path'; the first stage of the esoteric dimension of religion, preceding *ma'rifat* and *Haqîqat*.
tanbûr	Two- or three-stringed lute played especially for the sacred music of the Ahl-i Haqq.
tavakkul	Unshakeable inner confidence and trust in God.
Valî	God's 'viceroy' on earth, who exists in every age; a perfect human being who reflects the divine Essence.
zikr	A form of prayer involving the repetition of a sacred word or formula, such as some of the Names of God. It may be performed in a spiritual gathering or alone, in silence (*zikr khafî*), or chanted or sung out loud (*zikr jalî*).